Amazon CloudWatch Logs User Guide

A catalogue record for this book is available from the Hong Kong Public Libraries.

Published in Hong Kong by Samurai Media Limited.

Email: info@samuraimedia.org

ISBN 9789888408825

Contents

What is Amazon CloudWatch Logs?

You can use Amazon CloudWatch Logs to monitor, store, and access your log files from Amazon Elastic Compute Cloud (Amazon EC2) instances, AWS CloudTrail, Route 53, and other sources. You can then retrieve the associated log data from CloudWatch Logs.

Features

- **Monitor Logs from Amazon EC2 Instances in Real-time**—You can use CloudWatch Logs to monitor applications and systems using log data. For example, CloudWatch Logs can track the number of errors that occur in your application logs and send you a notification whenever the rate of errors exceeds a threshold you specify. CloudWatch Logs uses your log data for monitoring; so, no code changes are required. For example, you can monitor application logs for specific literal terms (such as "NullReferenceException") or count the number of occurrences of a literal term at a particular position in log data (such as "404" status codes in an Apache access log). When the term you are searching for is found, CloudWatch Logs reports the data to a CloudWatch metric that you specify. Log data is encrypted while in transit and while it is at rest. To get started, see Getting Started with CloudWatch Logs.
- **Monitor AWS CloudTrail Logged Events**—You can create alarms in CloudWatch and receive notifications of particular API activity as captured by CloudTrail and use the notification to perform troubleshooting. To get started, see Sending CloudTrail Events to CloudWatch Logs in the *AWS CloudTrail User Guide*.
- **Archive Log Data**—You can use CloudWatch Logs to store your log data in highly durable storage. You can change the log retention setting so that any log events older than this setting are automatically deleted. The CloudWatch Logs agent makes it easy to quickly send both rotated and non-rotated log data off of a host and into the log service. You can then access the raw log data when you need it.
- **Log Route 53 DNS Queries**—You can use CloudWatch Logs to log information about the DNS queries that Route 53 receives. For more information, see Logging DNS Queries in the *Amazon Route 53 Developer Guide*.

Related AWS Services

The following services are used in conjunction with CloudWatch Logs:

- **AWS CloudTrail** is a web service that enables you to monitor the calls made to the CloudWatch Logs API for your account, including calls made by the AWS Management Console, command line interface (CLI), and other services. When CloudTrail logging is turned on, CloudTrail captures API calls in your account and delivers the log files to the Amazon S3 bucket that you specify. Each log file can contain one or more records, depending on how many actions must be performed to satisfy a request. For more information about AWS CloudTrail, see What is AWS CloudTrail? in the *AWS CloudTrail User Guide*. For an example of the type of data that CloudWatch writes into CloudTrail log files, see Logging Amazon CloudWatch Logs API Calls in AWS CloudTrail.
- **AWS Identity and Access Management (IAM)** is a web service that helps you securely control access to AWS resources for your users. Use IAM to control who can use your AWS resources (authentication) and what resources they can use in which ways (authorization). For more information, see What is IAM? in the *IAM User Guide*.
- **Amazon Kinesis Data Streams** is a web service you can use for rapid and continuous data intake and aggregation. The type of data used includes IT infrastructure log data, application logs, social media, market data feeds, and web clickstream data. Because the response time for the data intake and processing is in real time, processing is typically lightweight. For more information, see What is Amazon Kinesis Data Streams? in the *Amazon Kinesis Data Streams Developer Guide*.
- **AWS Lambda** is a web service you can use to build applications that respond quickly to new information. Upload your application code as Lambda functions and Lambda runs your code on high-availability compute infrastructure and performs all the administration of the compute resources, including server and operating

system maintenance, capacity provisioning and automatic scaling, code and security patch deployment, and code monitoring and logging. All you need to do is supply your code in one of the languages that Lambda supports. For more information, see What is AWS Lambda? in the *AWS Lambda Developer Guide*.

Pricing

When you sign up for AWS, you can get started with CloudWatch Logs for free using the AWS Free Tier.

Standard rates apply for logs stored by other services using CloudWatch Logs (for example, Amazon VPC flow logs and Lambda logs).

For more information, see Amazon CloudWatch Pricing.

Amazon CloudWatch Logs Concepts

The terminology and concepts that are central to your understanding and use of CloudWatch Logs are described below.

Log Events

A log event is a record of some activity recorded by the application or resource being monitored. The log event record that CloudWatch Logs understands contains two properties: the timestamp of when the event occurred, and the raw event message. Event messages must be UTF-8 encoded.

Log Streams

A log stream is a sequence of log events that share the same source. More specifically, a log stream is generally intended to represent the sequence of events coming from the application instance or resource being monitored. For example, a log stream may be associated with an Apache access log on a specific host. When you no longer need a log stream, you can delete it using the aws logs delete-log-stream command. In addition, AWS may delete empty log streams that are over 2 months old.

Log Groups

Log groups define groups of log streams that share the same retention, monitoring, and access control settings. Each log stream has to belong to one log group. For example, if you have a separate log stream for the Apache access logs from each host, you could group those log streams into a single log group called MyWebsite.com/Apache/access_log.
There is no limit on the number of log streams that can belong to one log group.

Metric Filters

You can use metric filters to extract metric observations from ingested events and transform them to data points in a CloudWatch metric. Metric filters are assigned to log groups, and all of the filters assigned to a log group are applied to their log streams.

Retention Settings

Retention settings can be used to specify how long log events are kept in CloudWatch Logs. Expired log events get deleted automatically. Just like metric filters, retention settings are also assigned to log groups, and the retention assigned to a log group is applied to their log streams.

CloudWatch Logs Limits

CloudWatch Logs has the following limits:

Resource	Default Limit
Batch size	1 MB (maximum). This limit cannot be changed.
CreateLogGroup	5000 log groups/account/Region. If you exceed your log group limit, you get a `ResourceLimitExceeded` exception. You can request a limit increase.
Data archiving	Up to 5 GB of data archiving for free. This limit cannot be changed.
DescribeLogStreams	5 transactions per second (TPS/account/Region). If you experience frequent throttling, you can request a limit increase.
Event size	256 KB (maximum). This limit cannot be changed.
Export task	One active (running or pending) export task at a time, per account. This limit cannot be changed.
FilterLogEvents	5 transactions per second (TPS)/account/Region. This limit can be changed only in special circumstances. If you experience frequent throttling, contact AWS Support. For instructions, see AWS Service Limits.
GetLogEvents	10 requests per second per account per Region. We recommend subscriptions if you are continuously processing new data. If you need historical data, we recommend exporting your data to Amazon S3. This limit can be changed only in special circumstances. If you experience frequent throttling, contact AWS Support. For instructions, see AWS Service Limits.
Incoming data	Up to 5 GB of incoming data for free. This limit cannot be changed.
Log groups	5000 log groups per account per Region. You can request a limit increase. There is no limit on the number of log streams that can belong to one log group.
Metrics filters	100 per log group. This limit cannot be changed.

Resource	Default Limit
PutLogEvents	5 requests per second per log stream. Additional requests are throttled. This limit cannot be changed. The maximum batch size of a PutLogEvents request is 1MB. 1500 transactions per second per account per Region, except for the following Regions where the limit is 800 transactions per second per account per Region: ap-south-1, ap-northeast-1, ap-northeast-2, ap-southeast-1, ap-southeast-2, eu-central-1, eu-west-2, sa-east-1, us-east-2, and us-west-1. You can request a limit increase.
Subscription filters	1 per log group. This limit cannot be changed.

Getting Set Up

To use Amazon CloudWatch Logs you need an AWS account. Your AWS account allows you to use services (for example, Amazon EC2) to generate logs that you can view in the CloudWatch console, a web-based interface. In addition, you can install and configure the AWS Command Line Interface (AWS CLI).

Sign Up for Amazon Web Services (AWS)

When you create an AWS account, we automatically sign up your account for all AWS services. You pay only for the services that you use.

If you have an AWS account already, skip to the next step. If you don't have an AWS account, use the following procedure to create one.

To sign up for an AWS account

1. Open https://aws.amazon.com/, and then choose **Create an AWS Account**. **Note**
   This might be unavailable in your browser if you previously signed into the AWS Management Console. In that case, choose **Sign in to a different account**, and then choose **Create a new AWS account**.

2. Follow the online instructions.

   Part of the sign-up procedure involves receiving a phone call and entering a PIN using the phone keypad.

Sign in to the Amazon CloudWatch Console

To sign in to the Amazon CloudWatch console

1. Sign in to the AWS Management Console and open the CloudWatch console at https://console.aws.amazon.com/cloudwatch/.

2. If necessary, change the region. From the navigation bar, choose the region where you have your AWS resources.

3. In the navigation pane, choose **Logs**.

Set Up the Command Line Interface

You can use the AWS CLI to perform CloudWatch Logs operations.

For information about how to install and configure the AWS CLI, see Getting Set Up with the AWS Command Line Interface in the *AWS Command Line Interface User Guide*.

Getting Started with CloudWatch Logs

To collect logs from your Amazon EC2 instances and on-premises servers into CloudWatch Logs, AWS offers both a new unified CloudWatch agent, and an older CloudWatch Logs agent. We recommend the unified CloudWatch agent. The new unified agent has the following advantages.

- You can collect both logs and advanced metrics with the installation and configuration of just one agent.
- The unified agent enables the collection of logs from servers running Windows Server.
- If you are using the agent to collect CloudWatch metrics, the unified agent also enables the collection of additional system metrics, for in-guest visibility.
- The unified agent provides better performance.

The older CloudWatch Logs agent is still supported. If you are already using that agent, you may continue to do so. If you would like to migrate from the CloudWatch Logs agent to the new unified CloudWatch agent, we also provide a migration path.

Topics

- Use the Unified CloudWatch Agent to Get Started With CloudWatch Logs
- Use the Previous CloudWatch Logs Agent to Get Started With CloudWatch Logs
- Quick Start: Use AWS CloudFormation to Get Started With CloudWatch Logs

Differences between the two agents

The two agents provide similar functionality for CloudWatch Logs, with the unified CloudWatch agent adding the ability to collect logs from servers running Windows Server. The other difference is the symbols supported for log timestamp format, as shown in the following table.

Symbols Supported by Both Agents	Symbols Supported Only by Unified CloudWatch Agent	Symbols Supported Only by Older CloudWatch Logs Agent
%A, %a, %b, %B, %d, %H, %l, %m, %M, %p, %S, %y, %Y, %Z, %z	%-d, %-l, %-m, %-M, %-S	%c, %f, %j, %U, %W, %w

For more information about the meanings of the symbols supported by the new CloudWatch agent, see CloudWatch Agent Configuration File: Logs Section in the *Amazon CloudWatch User Guide*. For information about symbols supported by the CloudWatch Logs agent, see Agent Configuration File.

Use the Unified CloudWatch Agent to Get Started With CloudWatch Logs

For more information about using the unified CloudWatch agent to get started with CloudWatch Logs, see Collect Metrics and Logs from Amazon EC2 Instances and On-Premises Servers with the CloudWatch Agent in the *Amazon CloudWatch User Guide*. You complete the steps listed in this section to install, configure, and start the agent. If you are not using the agent to also collect CloudWatch metrics, you can ignore any sections that refer to metrics.

If you are currently using the older CloudWatch Logs agent and want to migrate to using the new unified agent, we recommend that you use the wizard included in the new agent package. This wizard can read your current CloudWatch Logs agent configuration file and set up the CloudWatch agent to collect the same logs. For more information about the wizard, see Create the CloudWatch Agent Configuration File with the Wizard in the *Amazon CloudWatch User Guide*.

Use the Previous CloudWatch Logs Agent to Get Started With CloudWatch Logs

Using the CloudWatch Logs agent, you can publish log data from Amazon EC2 instances running Linux or Windows Server, and logged events from AWS CloudTrail. We recommend instead using the CloudWatch unified agent to publish your log data. For more information about the new agent, see Collect Metrics and Logs from Amazon EC2 Instances and On-Premises Servers with the CloudWatch Agent in the *Amazon CloudWatch User Guide*. Alternatively, you can continue using the previous CloudWatch Logs agent.

Topics

- CloudWatch Logs Agent Prerequisites
- Quick Start: Install the Agent on a Running EC2 Linux Instance
- Quick Start: Install the Agent on an EC2 Linux Instance at Launch
- Quick Start: Install the Agent Using AWS OpsWorks
- Quick Start: Use CloudWatch Logs with Windows Server 2016 instances
- Quick Start: Use CloudWatch Logs with Windows Server 2012 and Windows Server 2008 instances
- Report the CloudWatch Logs Agent Status
- Start the CloudWatch Logs Agent
- Stop the CloudWatch Logs Agent

CloudWatch Logs Agent Prerequisites

The CloudWatch Logs agent requires Python version 2.7, 3.0, or 3.3, and any of the following versions of Linux:

- Amazon Linux version 2014.03.02 or later
- Ubuntu Server version 12.04, 14.04, or 16.04
- CentOS version 6, 6.3, 6.4, 6.5, or 7.0
- Red Hat Enterprise Linux (RHEL) version 6.5 or 7.0
- Debian 8.0

Quick Start: Install and Configure the CloudWatch Logs Agent on a Running EC2 Linux Instance

You can use the CloudWatch Logs agent installer on an existing EC2 instance to install and configure the CloudWatch Logs agent. After installation is complete, logs automatically flow from the instance to the log stream you create while installing the agent. The agent confirms that it has started and it stays running until you disable it.

In addition to using the agent, you can also publish log data using the AWS CLI, CloudWatch Logs SDK, or the CloudWatch Logs API. The AWS CLI is best suited for publishing data at the command line or through scripts. The CloudWatch Logs SDK is best suited for publishing log data directly from applications or building your own log publishing application.

Step 1: Configure Your IAM Role or User for CloudWatch Logs

The CloudWatch Logs agent supports IAM roles and users. If your instance already has an IAM role associated with it, make sure that you include the IAM policy below. If you don't already have an IAM role assigned to your instance, you can use your IAM credentials for the next steps or you can assign an IAM role to that instance. For more information, see Attaching an IAM Role to an Instance.

To configure your IAM role or user for CloudWatch Logs

1. Open the IAM console at https://console.aws.amazon.com/iam/.

2. In the navigation pane, choose **Roles**.

3. Choose the role by selecting the role name (do not select the check box next to the name).

4. On the **Permissions** tab, expand **Inline Policies** and choose the link to create an inline policy.

5. On the **Set Permissions** page, choose **Custom Policy**, **Select**.

   For more information about creating custom policies, see IAM Policies for Amazon EC2 in the *Amazon EC2 User Guide for Linux Instances*.

6. On the **Review Policy** page, for **Policy Name**, type a name for the policy.

7. For **Policy Document**, paste in the following policy:

```
 1 {
 2    "Version": "2012-10-17",
 3    "Statement": [
 4      {
 5        "Effect": "Allow",
 6        "Action": [
 7          "logs:CreateLogGroup",
 8          "logs:CreateLogStream",
 9          "logs:PutLogEvents",
10          "logs:DescribeLogStreams"
11      ],
12        "Resource": [
13          "arn:aws:logs:*:*:*"
14      ]
15    }
16  ]
17 }
```

8. Choose **Apply Policy**.

Step 2: Install and Configure CloudWatch Logs on an Existing Amazon EC2 Instance

The process for installing the CloudWatch Logs agent differs depending on whether your Amazon EC2 instance is running Amazon Linux, Ubuntu, CentOS, or Red Hat. Use the steps appropriate for the version of Linux on your instance.

To install and configure CloudWatch Logs on an existing Amazon Linux instance

Starting with Amazon Linux AMI 2014.09, the CloudWatch Logs agent is available as an RPM installation with the awslogs package. Earlier versions of Amazon Linux can access the awslogs package by updating their instance with the `sudo yum update -y` command. By installing the awslogs package as an RPM instead of the using the CloudWatch Logs installer, your instance receives regular package updates and patches from AWS without having to manually reinstall the CloudWatch Logs agent. **Warning**

Do not update the CloudWatch Logs agent using the RPM installation method if you previously used the Python script to install the agent. Doing so may cause configuration issues that prevent the CloudWatch Logs agent from sending your logs to CloudWatch.

1. Connect to your Amazon Linux instance. For more information, see Connect to Your Instance in the *Amazon EC2 User Guide for Linux Instances*.

   For more information about connection issues, see Troubleshooting Connecting to Your Instance in the *Amazon EC2 User Guide for Linux Instances*.

2. Update your Amazon Linux instance to pick up the latest changes in the package repositories.

   ```
   1 sudo yum update -y
   ```

3. Install the `awslogs` package. This is the recommended method for installing awslogs on Amazon Linux instances.

   ```
   1 sudo yum install -y awslogs
   ```

4. Edit the `/etc/awslogs/awslogs.conf` file to configure the logs to track. For more information about editing this file, see CloudWatch Logs Agent Reference.

5. By default, the `/etc/awslogs/awscli.conf` points to the us-east-1 region. To push your logs to a different region, edit the `awscli.conf` file and specify that region.

6. Start the `awslogs` service.

   ```
   1 sudo service awslogs start
   ```

   If you are running Amazon Linux 2, start the `awslogs` service with the following command.

   ```
   1 sudo systemctl start awslogsd
   ```

7. (Optional) Check the `/var/log/awslogs.log` file for errors logged when starting the service.

8. (Optional) Run the following command to start the `awslogs` service at each system boot.

   ```
   1 sudo chkconfig awslogs on
   ```

   If you are running Amazon Linux 2, start the `awslogs` service with the following command.

   ```
   1 sudo systemctl enable awslogsd.service
   ```

9. You should see the newly created log group and log stream in the CloudWatch console after the agent has been running for a few moments.

   For more information, see View Log Data Sent to CloudWatch Logs.

To install and configure CloudWatch Logs on an existing Ubuntu Server, CentOS, or Red Hat instance

If you're using an AMI running Ubuntu Server, CentOS, or Red Hat, use the following procedure to manually install the CloudWatch Logs agent on your instance.

1. Connect to your EC2 instance. For more information, see Connect to Your Instance in the *Amazon EC2 User Guide for Linux Instances*.

   For more information about connection issues, see Troubleshooting Connecting to Your Instance in the *Amazon EC2 User Guide for Linux Instances*.

2. Run the CloudWatch Logs agent installer using one of two options. You can run it directly from the internet, or download the files and run it standalone. **Note**
   If you are running CentOS 6.x, Red Hat 6.x, or Ubuntu 12.04, use the steps for downloading and running the installer standalone. Installing the CloudWatch Logs agent directly from the internet is not supported on these systems. **Note**
   On Ubuntu, run `apt-get update` before running the commands below.

   To run it directly from the internet, use the following commands and follow the prompts:

   ```
   1 curl https://s3.amazonaws.com/aws-cloudwatch/downloads/latest/awslogs-agent-setup.py -O
   ```

   ```
   1 sudo python ./awslogs-agent-setup.py --region us-east-1
   ```

   If the preceding command does not work, try the following:

   ```
   1 sudo python3 ./awslogs-agent-setup.py --region us-east-1
   ```

   To download and run it standalone, use the following commands and follow the prompts:

   ```
   1 curl https://s3.amazonaws.com/aws-cloudwatch/downloads/latest/awslogs-agent-setup.py -O
   ```

   ```
   1 curl https://s3.amazonaws.com/aws-cloudwatch/downloads/latest/AgentDependencies.tar.gz -O
   ```

   ```
   1 tar xvf AgentDependencies.tar.gz -C /tmp/
   ```

   ```
   1 sudo python ./awslogs-agent-setup.py --region us-east-1 --dependency-path /tmp/
       AgentDependencies
   ```

   You can install the CloudWatch Logs agent by specifying the us-east-1, us-west-1, us-west-2, ap-south-1, ap-northeast-2, ap-southeast-1, ap-southeast-2, ap-northeast-1, eu-central-1, eu-west-1, or sa-east-1 regions.
   Note
   For more information about the current version and the version history of `awslogs-agent-setup`, see CHANGELOG.txt.

   The CloudWatch Logs agent installer requires certain information during setup. Before you start, you need to know which log file to monitor and its time stamp format. You should also have the following information ready.
   [See the AWS documentation website for more details]

   After you have completed these steps, the installer asks about configuring another log file. You can run the process as many times as you like for each log file. If you have no more log files to monitor, choose **N** when prompted by the installer to set up another log. For more information about the settings in the agent configuration file, see CloudWatch Logs Agent Reference. **Note**
   Configuring multiple log sources to send data to a single log stream is not supported.

3. You should see the newly created log group and log stream in the CloudWatch console after the agent has been running for a few moments.

   For more information, see View Log Data Sent to CloudWatch Logs.

Quick Start: Install and Configure the CloudWatch Logs Agent on an EC2 Linux Instance at Launch

You can use Amazon EC2 user data, a feature of Amazon EC2 that allows parametric information to be passed to the instance on launch, to install and configure the CloudWatch Logs agent on that instance. To pass the CloudWatch Logs agent installation and configuration information to Amazon EC2, you can provide the configuration file in a network location such as an Amazon S3 bucket.

Configuring multiple log sources to send data to a single log stream is not supported.

Prerequisite
Create an agent configuration file that describes all your log groups and log streams. This is a text file that describes the log files to monitor as well as the log groups and log streams to upload them to. The agent consumes this configuration file and starts monitoring and uploading all the log files described in it. For more information about the settings in the agent configuration file, see CloudWatch Logs Agent Reference.

The following is a sample agent configuration file for Amazon Linux

```
1  [general]
2  state_file = /var/awslogs/state/agent-state
3
4  [/var/log/messages]
5  file = /var/log/messages
6  log_group_name = /var/log/messages
7  log_stream_name = {instance_id}
8  datetime_format = %b %d %H:%M:%S
```

The following is a sample agent configuration file for Ubuntu

```
1  [general]
2  state_file = /var/awslogs/state/agent-state
3
4  [/var/log/syslog]
5  file = /var/log/syslog
6  log_group_name = /var/log/syslog
7  log_stream_name = {instance_id}
8  datetime_format = %b %d %H:%M:%S
```

To configure your IAM role

1. Open the IAM console at https://console.aws.amazon.com/iam/.

2. In the navigation pane, choose **Policies, Create Policy**.

3. On the **Create Policy** page, for **Create Your Own Policy**, choose **Select**. For more information about creating custom policies, see IAM Policies for Amazon EC2 in the *Amazon EC2 User Guide for Linux Instances*.

4. On the **Review Policy** page, for **Policy Name**, type a name for the policy.

5. For **Policy Document**, paste in the following policy:

```
1  {
2      "Version": "2012-10-17",
3      "Statement": [
4          {
5              "Effect": "Allow",
6              "Action": [
7                  "logs:CreateLogGroup",
```

```
 8              "logs:CreateLogStream",
 9              "logs:PutLogEvents",
10              "logs:DescribeLogStreams"
11          ],
12          "Resource": [
13              "arn:aws:logs:*:*:*"
14          ]
15      },
16      {
17          "Effect": "Allow",
18          "Action": [
19              "s3:GetObject"
20          ],
21          "Resource": [
22              "arn:aws:s3:::myawsbucket/*"
23          ]
24      }
25   ]
26 }
```

6. Choose **Create Policy**.

7. In the navigation pane, choose **Roles**, **Create New Role**.

8. On the **Set Role Name** page, type a name for the role and then choose **Next Step**.

9. On the **Select Role Type** page, choose **Select** next to **Amazon EC2**.

10. On the **Attach Policy** page, in the table header, choose **Policy Type**, **Customer Managed**.

11. Select the IAM policy that you created and then choose **Next Step**.

12. Choose **Create Role**.

   For more information about IAM users and policies, see IAM Users and Groups and Managing IAM Policies in the *IAM User Guide.*

To launch a new instance and enable CloudWatch Logs

1. Open the Amazon EC2 console at https://console.aws.amazon.com/ec2/.

2. Choose **Launch Instance**.

   For more information, see Launching an Instance in *Amazon EC2 User Guide for Linux Instances.*

3. On the **Step 1: Choose an Amazon Machine Image (AMI)** page, select the Linux instance type to launch, and then on the **Step 2: Choose an Instance Type** page, choose **Next: Configure Instance Details**.

   Make sure that cloud-init is included in your Amazon Machine Image (AMI). Amazon Linux AMIs, and AMIs for Ubuntu and RHEL already include cloud-init, but CentOS and other AMIs in the AWS Marketplace might not.

4. On the **Step 3: Configure Instance Details** page, for **IAM role**, select the IAM role that you created.

5. Under **Advanced Details**, for **User data**, paste the following script into the box. Then update that script by changing the value of the **-c** option to the location of your agent configuration file:

```
1 #!/bin/bash
2 curl https://s3.amazonaws.com//aws-cloudwatch/downloads/latest/awslogs-agent-setup.py -O
3 chmod +x ./awslogs-agent-setup.py
4 ./awslogs-agent-setup.py -n -r us-east-1 -c s3://myawsbucket/my-config-file
```

6. Make any other changes to the instance, review your launch settings, and then choose **Launch**.

7. You should see the newly created log group and log stream in the CloudWatch console after the agent has been running for a few moments.

   For more information, see View Log Data Sent to CloudWatch Logs.

Quick Start: Install the CloudWatch Logs Agent Using AWS OpsWorks and Chef

You can install the CloudWatch Logs agent and create log streams using AWS OpsWorks and Chef, which is a third-party systems and cloud infrastructure automation tool. Chef uses "recipes," which you write to install and configure software on your computer, and "cookbooks," which are collections of recipes, to perform its configuration and policy distribution tasks. For more information, see Chef.

The Chef recipes examples below show how to monitor one log file on each EC2 instance. The recipes use the stack name as the log group and the instance's hostname as the log stream name. To monitor multiple log files, you need to extend the recipes to create multiple log groups and log streams.

Step 1: Create Custom Recipes

Create a repository to store your recipes. AWS OpsWorks supports Git and Subversion, or you can store an archive in Amazon S3. The structure of your cookbook repository is described in Cookbook Repositories in the *AWS OpsWorks User Guide*. The examples below assume that the cookbook is named `logs`. The install.rb recipe installs the CloudWatch Logs agent. You can also download the cookbook example (CloudWatchLogs-Cookbooks.zip).

Create a file named metadata.rb that contains the following code:

```
1 #metadata.rb
2
3 name            'logs'
4 version         '0.0.1'
```

Create the CloudWatch Logs configuration file:

```
1 #config.rb
2
3 template "/tmp/cwlogs.cfg" do
4   cookbook "logs"
5   source "cwlogs.cfg.erb"
6   owner "root"
7   group "root"
8   mode 0644
9 end
```

Download and install the CloudWatch Logs agent:

```
1 # install.rb
2
3 directory "/opt/aws/cloudwatch" do
4   recursive true
5 end
6
7 remote_file "/opt/aws/cloudwatch/awslogs-agent-setup.py" do
8   source "https://s3.amazonaws.com//aws-cloudwatch/downloads/latest/awslogs-agent-setup.py"
9   mode "0755"
10 end
11
12   execute "Install CloudWatch Logs agent" do
13   command "/opt/aws/cloudwatch/awslogs-agent-setup.py -n -r region -c /tmp/cwlogs.cfg"
14   not_if { system "pgrep -f aws-logs-agent-setup" }
15 end
```

Note

In the above example, replace *region* with one of the following: us-east-1, us-west-1, us-west-2, ap-south-1, ap-northeast-2, ap-southeast-1, ap-southeast-2, ap-northeast-1, eu-central-1, eu-west-1, or sa-east-1.

If the installation of the agent fails, check to make sure that the `python-dev` package is installed. If it isn't, use the following command, and then retry the agent installation:

```
1 sudo apt-get -y install python-dev
```

This recipe uses a cwlogs.cfg.erb template file that you can modify to specify various attributes such as what files to log. For more information about these attributes, see CloudWatch Logs Agent Reference.

```
1 [general]
2 # Path to the AWSLogs agent's state file. Agent uses this file to maintain
3 # client side state across its executions.
4 state_file = /var/awslogs/state/agent-state
5
6
7 ## Each log file is defined in its own section. The section name doesn't
8 ## matter as long as its unique within this file.
9 #
10 #[kern.log]
11 #
12 ## Path of log file for the agent to monitor and upload.
13 #
14 #file = /var/log/kern.log
15 #
16 ## Name of the destination log group.
17 #
18 #log_group_name = kern.log
19 #
20 ## Name of the destination log stream.
21 #
22 #log_stream_name = {instance_id}
23 #
24 ## Format specifier for timestamp parsing.
25 #
26 #datetime_format = %b %d %H:%M:%S
27 #
28 #
29
30 [<%= node[:opsworks][:stack][:name] %>]
31 datetime_format - [%Y %m %d %H:%M:%S]
32 log_group_name = <%= node[:opsworks][:stack][:name].gsub(' ','_') %>
33 file = <%= node[:cwlogs][:logfile] %>
34 log_stream_name = <%= node[:opsworks][:instance][:hostname] %>
```

The template gets the stack name and host name by referencing the corresponding attributes in the stack configuration and deployment JSON. The attribute that specifies the file to log is defined in the cwlogs cookbook's default.rb attributes file (logs/attributes/default.rb).

```
1 default[:cwlogs][:logfile] = '/var/log/aws/opsworks/opsworks-agent.statistics.log'
```

Step 2: Create an AWS OpsWorks Stack

1. Open the AWS OpsWorks console at https://console.aws.amazon.com/opsworks/.

2. On the **OpsWorks Dashboard**, choose **Add stack** to create an AWS OpsWorks stack.

3. On the **Add stack** screen, choose **Chef 11 stack**.

4. For **Stack name**, enter a name.

5. For **Use custom Chef Cookbooks**, choose **Yes**.

6. For **Repository type**, select the repository type that you use. If you're using the above example, choose **Http Archive**.

7. For **Repository URL**, enter the repository where you stored the cookbook that you created in the previous step. If you're using the above example, enter **https://s3/.amazonaws/.com//aws/-cloudwatch/ downloads/CloudWatchLogs/-Cookbooks/.zip**/.

8. Choose **Add Stack** to create the stack.

Step 3: Extend Your IAM Role

To use CloudWatch Logs with your AWS OpsWorks instances, you need to extend the IAM role used by your instances.

1. Open the IAM console at https://console.aws.amazon.com/iam/.

2. In the navigation pane, choose **Policies, Create Policy**.

3. On the **Create Policy** page, under **Create Your Own Policy**, choose **Select**. For more information about creating custom policies, see IAM Policies for Amazon EC2 in the *Amazon EC2 User Guide for Linux Instances*.

4. On the **Review Policy** page, for **Policy Name**, type a name for the policy.

5. For **Policy Document**, paste in the following policy:

```
1  {
2    "Version": "2012-10-17",
3    "Statement": [
4      {
5        "Effect": "Allow",
6        "Action": [
7          "logs:CreateLogGroup",
8          "logs:CreateLogStream",
9          "logs:PutLogEvents",
10         "logs:DescribeLogStreams"
11       ],
12       "Resource": [
13       "arn:aws:logs:*:*:*"
14       ]
15     }
16   ]
17 }
```

6. Choose **Create Policy**.

7. In the navigation pane, choose **Roles**, and then in the contents pane, for **Role Name**, select the name of the instance role used by your AWS OpsWorks stack. You can find the one used by your stack in the stack settings (the default is `aws-opsworks-ec2-role`). **Note** Choose the role name, not the check box.

8. On the **Permissions** tab, under **Managed Policies**, choose **Attach Policy**.

9. On the **Attach Policy** page, in the table header (next to **Filter** and **Search**), choose **Policy Type, Customer Managed Policies**.

10. For **Customer Managed Policies**, select the IAM policy that you created above and choose **Attach Policy**.

For more information about IAM users and policies, see IAM Users and Groups and Managing IAM Policies in the *IAM User Guide*.

Step 4: Add a Layer

1. Open the AWS OpsWorks console at https://console.aws.amazon.com/opsworks/.

2. In the navigation pane, choose **Layers**.

3. In the contents pane, select a layer and choose **Add layer**.

4. On the **OpsWorks** tab, for **Layer type**, choose **Custom**.

5. For the **Name** and **Short name** fields, enter the long and short name for the layer, and then choose **Add layer**.

6. On the **Recipes** tab, under **Custom Chef Recipes**, there are several headings—*Setup, Configure, Deploy, Undeploy,* and *Shutdown*—that correspond to AWS OpsWorks lifecycle events. AWS OpsWorks triggers these events at these key points in instance's lifecycle, which runs the associated recipes. **Note** If the above headings aren't visible, under **Custom Chef Recipes**, choose **edit**.

7. Enter *logs::config, logs::install* next to **Setup**, choose + to add it to the list, and then choose **Save**.

AWS OpsWorks runs this recipe on each of the new instances in this layer, right after the instance boots.

Step 5: Add an Instance

The layer only controls how to configure instances. You now need to add some instances to the layer and start them.

1. Open the AWS OpsWorks console at https://console.aws.amazon.com/opsworks/.

2. In the navigation pane, choose **Instances** and then under your layer, choose + **Instance**.

3. Accept the default settings and choose **Add Instance** to add the instance to the layer.

4. In the row's **Actions** column, click **start** to start the instance.

AWS OpsWorks launches a new EC2 instance and configures CloudWatch Logs. The instance's status changes to online when it's ready.

Step 6: View Your Logs

You should see the newly created log group and log stream in the CloudWatch console after the agent has been running for a few moments.

For more information, see View Log Data Sent to CloudWatch Logs.

Quick Start: Enable Your Amazon EC2 Instances Running Windows Server 2016 to Send Logs to CloudWatch Logs Using the CloudWatch Logs Agent

There are multiple methods you can use to enable instances running Windows Server 2016 to send logs to CloudWatch Logs. The steps in this section use Systems Manager Run Command. For information about the other possible methods, see Sending Logs, Events, and Performance Counters to Amazon CloudWatch.

Topics

- Download the Sample Configuration File
- Configure the JSON File for CloudWatch
- Create an IAM User and Role for Systems Manager
- Verify Systems Manager Prerequisites
- Verify Internet Access
- Enable CloudWatch Logs Using Systems Manager Run Command

Download the Sample Configuration File

Download the following sample file to your computer: AWS.EC2.Windows.CloudWatch.json.

Configure the JSON File for CloudWatch

You determine which logs to send to CloudWatch by specifying your choices in a configuration file. The process of creating this file and specifying your choices can take 30 minutes or more to complete. After you have completed this task once, you can reuse the configuration file on all of your instances.

Topics

- Step 1: Enable CloudWatch Logs
- Step 2: Configure Settings for CloudWatch
- Step 3: Configure the Data to Send
- Step 4: Configure Flow Control
- Step 5: Save JSON Content

Step 1: Enable CloudWatch Logs

At the top of the JSON file, change "false" to "true" for `IsEnabled`:

```
1 "IsEnabled": true,
```

Step 2: Configure Settings for CloudWatch

Specify credentials, region, a log group name, and a log stream namespace. This enables the instance to send log data to CloudWatch Logs. To send the same log data to different locations, you can add additional sections with unique IDs (for example, "CloudWatchLogs2" and CloudWatchLogs3") and a different region for each ID.

To configure settings to send log data to CloudWatch Logs

1. In the JSON file, locate the `CloudWatchLogs` section.

```
1 {
2     "Id": "CloudWatchLogs",
3     "FullName": "AWS.EC2.Windows.CloudWatch.CloudWatchLogsOutput,AWS.EC2.Windows.CloudWatch
        ",
4     "Parameters": {
5         "AccessKey": "",
6         "SecretKey": "",
7         "Region": "us-east-1",
8         "LogGroup": "Default-Log-Group",
9         "LogStream": "{instance_id}"
10    }
11 },
```

2. Leave the `AccessKey` and `SecretKey` field blank. Youconfigure credentials using an IAM role.

3. For `Region`, type the region to which to send log data (for example, `us-east-2`).

4. For `LogGroup`, type the name for your log group. This name appears on the **Log Groups** screen in the CloudWatch console.

5. For `LogStream`, type the destination log stream. This name appears on the **Log Groups > Streams** screen in the CloudWatch console.

   If you use `{instance_id}`, the default, the log stream name is the instance ID of this instance.

   If you specify a log stream name that doesn't already exist, CloudWatch Logs automatically creates it for you. You can define a log stream name using a literal string, the predefined variables `{instance_id}`, `{hostname}`, and `{ip_address}`, or a combination of these.

Step 3: Configure the Data to Send

You can send event log data, Event Tracing for Windows (ETW) data, and other log data to CloudWatch Logs.

To send Windows application event log data to CloudWatch Logs

1. In the JSON file, locate the `ApplicationEventLog` section.

```
1 {
2     "Id": "ApplicationEventLog",
3     "FullName": "AWS.EC2.Windows.CloudWatch.EventLog.EventLogInputComponent,AWS.EC2.Windows
        .CloudWatch",
4     "Parameters": {
5         "LogName": "Application",
6         "Levels": "1"
7     }
8 },
```

2. For `Levels`, specify the type of messages to upload. You can specify one of the following values:

   - **1** - Upload only error messages.
   - **2** - Upload only warning messages.
   - **4** - Upload only information messages.

   You can combine values to include more than one type of message. For example, a value of **3** uploads error messages (**1**) and warning messages (**2**). A value of **7** uploads error messages (**1**), warning messages (**2**), and information messages (**4**).

To send security log data to CloudWatch Logs

1. In the JSON file, locate the `SecurityEventLog` section.

```
1 {
2     "Id": "SecurityEventLog",
3     "FullName": "AWS.EC2.Windows.CloudWatch.EventLog.EventLogInputComponent,AWS.EC2.Windows
        .CloudWatch",
4     "Parameters": {
5         "LogName": "Security",
6         "Levels": "7"
7     }
8 },
```

2. For `Levels`, type **7** to upload all messages.

To send system event log data to CloudWatch Logs

1. In the JSON file, locate the `SystemEventLog` section.

```
1 {
2     "Id": "SystemEventLog",
3     "FullName": "AWS.EC2.Windows.CloudWatch.EventLog.EventLogInputComponent,AWS.EC2.Windows
        .CloudWatch",
4     "Parameters": {
5         "LogName": "System",
6         "Levels": "7"
7     }
8 },
```

2. For `Levels`, specify the type of messages to upload. You can specify one of the following values:

   - **1** - Upload only error messages.
   - **2** - Upload only warning messages.
   - **4** - Upload only information messages.

   You can combine values to include more than one type of message. For example, a value of **3** uploads error messages (**1**) and warning messages (**2**). A value of **7** uploads error messages (**1**), warning messages (**2**), and information messages (**4**).

To send other types of event log data to CloudWatch Logs

1. In the JSON file, add a new section. Each section must have a unique `Id`.

```
1 {
2     "Id": "Id-name",
3     "FullName": "AWS.EC2.Windows.CloudWatch.EventLog.EventLogInputComponent,AWS.EC2.Windows
        .CloudWatch",
4     "Parameters": {
5         "LogName": "Log-name",
6         "Levels": "7"
7     }
8 },
```

2. For `Id`, type a name for the log to upload (for example, **WindowsBackup**).

3. For `LogName`, type the name of the log to upload. You can find the name of the log as follows.

   1. Open Event Viewer.

   2. In the navigation pane, choose **Applications and Services Logs**.

   3. Navigate to the log, and then choose **Actions**, **Properties**.

4. For `Levels`, specify the type of messages to upload. You can specify one of the following values:

- **1** - Upload only error messages.
- **2** - Upload only warning messages.
- **4** - Upload only information messages.

You can combine values to include more than one type of message. For example, a value of **3** uploads error messages (**1**) and warning messages (**2**). A value of **7** uploads error messages (**1**), warning messages (**2**), and information messages (**4**).

To send Event Tracing for Windows data to CloudWatch Logs

ETW (Event Tracing for Windows) provides an efficient and detailed logging mechanism that applications can write logs to. Each ETW is controlled by a session manager that can start and stop the logging session. Each session has a provider and one or more consumers.

1. In the JSON file, locate the ETW section.

```
1  {
2      "Id": "ETW",
3      "FullName": "AWS.EC2.Windows.CloudWatch.EventLog.EventLogInputComponent,AWS.EC2.Windows
           .CloudWatch",
4      "Parameters": {
5          "LogName": "Microsoft-Windows-WinINet/Analytic",
6          "Levels": "7"
7      }
8  },
```

2. For `LogName`, type the name of the log to upload.

3. For `Levels`, specify the type of messages to upload. You can specify one of the following values:

- **1** - Upload only error messages.
- **2** - Upload only warning messages.
- **4** - Upload only information messages.

You can combine values to include more than one type of message. For example, a value of **3** uploads error messages (**1**) and warning messages (**2**). A value of **7** uploads error messages (**1**), warning messages (**2**), and information messages (**4**).

To send custom logs (any text-based log file) to CloudWatch Logs

1. In the JSON file, locate the `CustomLogs` section.

```
1  {
2      "Id": "CustomLogs",
3      "FullName": "AWS.EC2.Windows.CloudWatch.CustomLog.CustomLogInputComponent,AWS.EC2.
           Windows.CloudWatch",
4      "Parameters": [
5          "LogDirectoryPath": "C:\\CustomLogs\\",
6          "TimestampFormat": "MM/dd/yyyy HH:mm:ss",
7          "Encoding": "UTF-8",
8          "Filter": "",
9          "CultureName": "en-US",
10         "TimeZoneKind": "Local",
11         "LineCount": "5"
12     }
13 },
```

2. For `LogDirectoryPath`, type the path where logs are stored on your instance.

3. For `TimestampFormat`, type the time stamp format to use. For more information about supported values, see the Custom Date and Time Format Strings topic on MSDN. **Important**

Your source log file must have the time stamp at the beginning of each log line and there must be a space following the time stamp.

4. For `Encoding`, type the file encoding to use (for example, UTF-8). For a list of supported values, see the Encoding Class topic on MSDN. **Note**
Use the encoding name, not the display name.

5. (Optional) For `Filter`, type the prefix of log names. Leave this parameter blank to monitor all files. For more information about supported values, see the FileSystemWatcherFilter Property topic on MSDN.

6. (Optional) For `CultureName`, type the locale where the time stamp is logged. If `CultureName` is blank, it defaults to the same locale currently used by your Windows instance. For more information about, see the **Language tag** column in the table in the Product Behavior topic on MSDN. **Note**
The `div`, `div-MV`, `hu`, and `hu-HU` values are not supported.

7. (Optional) For `TimeZoneKind`, type `Local` or `UTC`. You can set this to provide time zone information when no time zone information is included in your log's time stamp. If this parameter is left blank and if your time stamp doesn't include time zone information, CloudWatch Logs defaults to the local time zone. This parameter is ignored if your time stamp already contains time zone information.

8. (Optional) For `LineCount`, type the number of lines in the header to identify the log file. For example, IIS log files have virtually identical headers. You could enter **5**, which would read the first three lines of the log file header to identify it. In IIS log files, the third line is the date and time stamp, but the time stamp is not always guaranteed to be different between log files. For this reason, we recommend including at least one line of actual log data to uniquely fingerprint the log file.

To send IIS log data to CloudWatch Logs

1. In the JSON file, locate the `IISLog` section.

```
1  {
2      "Id": "IISLogs",
3      "FullName": "AWS.EC2.Windows.CloudWatch.CustomLog.CustomLogInputComponent,AWS.EC2.
           Windows.CloudWatch",
4      "Parameters": {
5          "LogDirectoryPath": "C:\\inetpub\\logs\\LogFiles\\W3SVC1",
6          "TimestampFormat": "yyyy-MM-dd HH:mm:ss",
7          "Encoding": "UTF-8",
8          "Filter": "",
9          "CultureName": "en-US",
10         "TimeZoneKind": "UTC",
11         "LineCount": "5"
12     }
13 },
```

2. For `LogDirectoryPath`, type the folder where IIS logs are stored for an individual site (for example, C:\inetpub\logs\LogFiles\W3SVCn). **Note**
Only W3C log format is supported. IIS, NCSA, and Custom formats are not supported.

3. For `TimestampFormat`, type the time stamp format to use. For more information about supported values, see the Custom Date and Time Format Strings topic on MSDN.

4. For `Encoding`, type the file encoding to use (for example, UTF-8). For more information about supported values, see the Encoding Class topic on MSDN. **Note**
Use the encoding name, not the display name.

5. (Optional) For `Filter`, type the prefix of log names. Leave this parameter blank to monitor all files. For more information about supported values, see the FileSystemWatcherFilter Property topic on MSDN.

6. (Optional) For `CultureName`, type the locale where the time stamp is logged. If `CultureName` is blank, it defaults to the same locale currently used by your Windows instance. For more information about

supported values, see the `Language tag` column in the table in the Product Behavior topic on MSDN.
Note
The `div`, `div-MV`, `hu`, and `hu-HU` values are not supported.

7. (Optional) For `TimeZoneKind`, enter `Local` or `UTC`. You can set this to provide time zone information when no time zone information is included in your log's time stamp. If this parameter is left blank and if your time stamp doesn't include time zone information, CloudWatch Logs defaults to the local time zone. This parameter is ignored if your time stamp already contains time zone information.

8. (Optional) For `LineCount`, type the number of lines in the header to identify the log file. For example, IIS log files have virtually identical headers. You could enter **5**, which would read the first five lines of the log file's header to identify it. In IIS log files, the third line is the date and time stamp, but the time stamp is not always guaranteed to be different between log files. For this reason, we recommend including at least one line of actual log data for uniquely fingerprinting the log file.

Step 4: Configure Flow Control

Each data type must have a corresponding destination in the `Flows` section. For example, to send the custom log, ETW log, and system log to CloudWatch Logs, add `(CustomLogs,ETW,SystemEventLog),CloudWatchLogs` to the `Flows` section.

Warning
Adding a step that is not valid blocks the flow. For example, if you add a disk metric step, but your instance doesn't have a disk, all steps in the flow are blocked.

You can send the same log file to more than one destination. For example, to send the application log to two different destinations that you defined in the `CloudWatchLogs` section, add `ApplicationEventLog,(CloudWatchLogs,CloudWatchLogs2)` to the `Flows` section.

To configure flow control

1. In the `AWS.EC2.Windows.CloudWatch.json` file, locate the `Flows` section.

```
1  "Flows": {
2      "Flows": [
3        "PerformanceCounter,CloudWatch",
4        "(PerformanceCounter,PerformanceCounter2), CloudWatch2",
5        "(CustomLogs, ETW, SystemEventLog),CloudWatchLogs",
6        "CustomLogs, CloudWatchLogs2",
7        "ApplicationEventLog,(CloudWatchLogs, CloudWatchLogs2)"
8      ]
9  }
```

2. For `Flows`, add each data type that is to be uploaded (for example, `ApplicationEventLog`) and its destination (for example, `CloudWatchLogs`).

Step 5: Save JSON Content

You are now finished editing the JSON file. Save it, and paste the file contents into a text editor in another window. You will need the file contents in a later step of this procedure.

Create an IAM User and Role for Systems Manager

An IAM role for instance credentials is required when you use Systems Manager Run Command. This role enables Systems Manager to perform actions on the instance. You can optionally create a unique IAM user account for configuring and running Systems Manager. For more information, see Configuring Security Roles for

31

Systems Manager in the *AWS Systems Manager User Guide*. For information about how to attach an IAM role to an existing instance, see Attaching an IAM Role to an Instance in the *Amazon EC2 User Guide for Windows Instances*.

Verify Systems Manager Prerequisites

Before you use Systems Manager Run Command to configure integration with CloudWatch Logs, verify that your instances meet the minimum requirements. For more information, see Systems Manager Prerequisites in the *AWS Systems Manager User Guide*.

Verify Internet Access

Your Amazon EC2 Windows Server instances and managed instances must have outbound internet access in order to send log and event data to CloudWatch. For more information about how to configure internet access, see Internet Gateways in the *Amazon VPC User Guide*.

Enable CloudWatch Logs Using Systems Manager Run Command

Run Command enables you to manage the configuration of your instances on demand. You specify a Systems Manager document, specify parameters, and execute the command on one or more instances. The SSM agent on the instance processes the command and configures the instance as specified.

To configure integration with CloudWatch Logs using Run Command

1. Open the Amazon EC2 console at https://console.aws.amazon.com/ec2/.

2. In the navigation pane, choose **Systems Manager Services**, **Run Command**.

3. Choose **Run a command**.

4. For **Command document**, choose **AWS-ConfigureCloudWatch**.

5. For **Target instances**, choose the instances to integrate with CloudWatch Logs. If you do not see an instance in this list, it might not be configured for Run Command. For more information, see Systems Manager Prerequisites in the *Amazon EC2 User Guide for Windows Instances*.

6. For **Status**, choose **Enabled**.

7. For **Properties**, copy and paste the JSON content you created in the previous tasks.

8. Complete the remaining optional fields and choose **Run**.

Use the following procedure to view the results of command execution in the Amazon EC2 console.

To view command output in the console

1. Select a command.

2. Choose the **Output** tab.

3. Choose **View Output**. The command output page shows the results of your command execution.

Quick Start: Enable Your Amazon EC2 Instances Running Windows Server 2012 and Windows Server 2008 to Send logs to CloudWatch Logs

Use the following steps to enable your instances running Windows Server 2012 and Windows Server 2008 to send logs to CloudWatch Logs.

Download the Sample Configuration File

Download the following sample JSON file to your computer: AWS.EC2.Windows.CloudWatch.json. You edit it in the following steps.

Configure the JSON File for CloudWatch

You determine which logs to send to CloudWatch by specifying your choices in the JSON configuration file. The process of creating this file and specifying your choices can take 30 minutes or more to complete. After you have completed this task once, you can reuse the configuration file on all of your instances.

Topics

- Step 1: Enable CloudWatch Logs
- Step 2: Configure Settings for CloudWatch
- Step 3: Configure the Data to Send
- Step 4: Configure Flow Control

Step 1: Enable CloudWatch Logs

At the top of the JSON file, change "false" to "true" for `IsEnabled`:

```
1 "IsEnabled": true,
```

Step 2: Configure Settings for CloudWatch

Specify credentials, region, a log group name, and a log stream namespace. This enables the instance to send log data to CloudWatch Logs. To send the same log data to different locations, you can add additional sections with unique IDs (for example, "CloudWatchLogs2" and CloudWatchLogs3") and a different region for each ID.

To configure settings to send log data to CloudWatch Logs

1. In the JSON file, locate the `CloudWatchLogs` section.

```
1  {
2      "Id": "CloudWatchLogs",
3      "FullName": "AWS.EC2.Windows.CloudWatch.CloudWatchLogsOutput,AWS.EC2.Windows.CloudWatch
           ",
4      "Parameters": {
5          "AccessKey": "",
6          "SecretKey": "",
7          "Region": "us-east-1",
8          "LogGroup": "Default-Log-Group",
9          "LogStream": "{instance_id}"
10     }
11 },
```

2. Leave the `AccessKey` and `SecretKey` field blank. You configure credentials using an IAM role.

3. For `Region`, type the region to which to send log data (for example, `us-east-2`).

4. For `LogGroup`, type the name for your log group. This name appears on the **Log Groups** screen in the CloudWatch console.

5. For `LogStream`, type the destination log stream. This name appears on the **Log Groups > Streams** screen in the CloudWatch console.

   If you use `{instance_id}`, the default, the log stream name is the instance ID of this instance.

   If you specify a log stream name that doesn't already exist, CloudWatch Logs automatically creates it for you. You can define a log stream name using a literal string, the predefined variables `{instance_id}`, `{hostname}`, and `{ip_address}`, or a combination of these.

Step 3: Configure the Data to Send

You can send event log data, Event Tracing for Windows (ETW) data, and other log data to CloudWatch Logs.

To send Windows application event log data to CloudWatch Logs

1. In the JSON file, locate the `ApplicationEventLog` section.

```
1  {
2      "Id": "ApplicationEventLog",
3      "FullName": "AWS.EC2.Windows.CloudWatch.EventLog.EventLogInputComponent,AWS.EC2.Windows
           .CloudWatch",
4      "Parameters": {
5          "LogName": "Application",
6          "Levels": "1"
7      }
8  },
```

2. For `Levels`, specify the type of messages to upload. You can specify one of the following values:

   - **1** - Upload only error messages.
   - **2** - Upload only warning messages.
   - **4** - Upload only information messages.

   You can combine values to include more than one type of message. For example, a value of **3** uploads error messages (**1**) and warning messages (**2**). A value of **7** uploads error messages (**1**), warning messages (**2**), and information messages (**4**).

To send security log data to CloudWatch Logs

1. In the JSON file, locate the `SecurityEventLog` section.

```
1  {
2      "Id": "SecurityEventLog",
3      "FullName": "AWS.EC2.Windows.CloudWatch.EventLog.EventLogInputComponent,AWS.EC2.Windows
           .CloudWatch",
4      "Parameters": {
5          "LogName": "Security",
6          "Levels": "7"
7      }
8  },
```

2. For `Levels`, type **7** to upload all messages.

To send system event log data to CloudWatch Logs

1. In the JSON file, locate the `SystemEventLog` section.

```
1 {
2     "Id": "SystemEventLog",
3     "FullName": "AWS.EC2.Windows.CloudWatch.EventLog.EventLogInputComponent,AWS.EC2.Windows
          .CloudWatch",
4     "Parameters": {
5         "LogName": "System",
6         "Levels": "7"
7     }
8 },
```

2. For `Levels`, specify the type of messages to upload. You can specify one of the following values:

   - **1** - Upload only error messages.
   - **2** - Upload only warning messages.
   - **4** - Upload only information messages.

   You can combine values to include more than one type of message. For example, a value of **3** uploads error messages (**1**) and warning messages (**2**). A value of **7** uploads error messages (**1**), warning messages (**2**), and information messages (**4**).

To send other types of event log data to CloudWatch Logs

1. In the JSON file, add a new section. Each section must have a unique `Id`.

```
1 {
2     "Id": "Id-name",
3     "FullName": "AWS.EC2.Windows.CloudWatch.EventLog.EventLogInputComponent,AWS.EC2.Windows
          .CloudWatch",
4     "Parameters": {
5         "LogName": "Log-name",
6         "Levels": "7"
7     }
8 },
```

2. For `Id`, type a name for the log to upload (for example, **WindowsBackup**).

3. For `LogName`, type the name of the log to upload. You can find the name of the log as follows.

   1. Open Event Viewer.

   2. In the navigation pane, choose **Applications and Services Logs**.

   3. Navigate to the log, and then choose **Actions**, **Properties**.

4. For `Levels`, specify the type of messages to upload. You can specify one of the following values:

   - **1** - Upload only error messages.
   - **2** - Upload only warning messages.
   - **4** - Upload only information messages.

   You can combine values to include more than one type of message. For example, a value of **3** uploads error messages (**1**) and warning messages (**2**). A value of **7** uploads error messages (**1**), warning messages (**2**), and information messages (**4**).

To send Event Tracing for Windows data to CloudWatch Logs

ETW (Event Tracing for Windows) provides an efficient and detailed logging mechanism that applications can write logs to. Each ETW is controlled by a session manager that can start and stop the logging session. Each session has a provider and one or more consumers.

1. In the JSON file, locate the `ETW` section.

```
1  {
2      "Id": "ETW",
3      "FullName": "AWS.EC2.Windows.CloudWatch.EventLog.EventLogInputComponent,AWS.EC2.Windows
           .CloudWatch",
4      "Parameters": {
5          "LogName": "Microsoft-Windows-WinINet/Analytic",
6          "Levels": "7"
7      }
8  },
```

2. For `LogName`, type the name of the log to upload.

3. For `Levels`, specify the type of messages to upload. You can specify one of the following values:

   - **1** - Upload only error messages.
   - **2** - Upload only warning messages.
   - **4** - Upload only information messages.

   You can combine values to include more than one type of message. For example, a value of **3** uploads error messages (**1**) and warning messages (**2**). A value of **7** uploads error messages (**1**), warning messages (**2**), and information messages (**4**).

To send custom logs (any text-based log file) to CloudWatch Logs

1. In the JSON file, locate the `CustomLogs` section.

```
1  {
2      "Id": "CustomLogs",
3      "FullName": "AWS.EC2.Windows.CloudWatch.CustomLog.CustomLogInputComponent,AWS.EC2.
           Windows.CloudWatch",
4      "Parameters": {
5          "LogDirectoryPath": "C:\\CustomLogs\\",
6          "TimestampFormat": "MM/dd/yyyy HH:mm:ss",
7          "Encoding": "UTF-8",
8          "Filter": "",
9          "CultureName": "en-US",
10         "TimeZoneKind": "Local",
11         "LineCount": "5"
12     }
13 },
```

2. For `LogDirectoryPath`, type the path where logs are stored on your instance.

3. For `TimestampFormat`, type the time stamp format to use. For more information about supported values, see the Custom Date and Time Format Strings topic on MSDN. **Important**
Your source log file must have the time stamp at the beginning of each log line and there must be a space following the time stamp.

4. For `Encoding`, type the file encoding to use (for example, UTF-8). For more information about supported values, see the Encoding Class topic on MSDN. **Note**
Use the encoding name, not the display name.

5. (Optional) For `Filter`, type the prefix of log names. Leave this parameter blank to monitor all files. For more information about supported values, see the FileSystemWatcherFilter Property topic on MSDN.

6. (Optional) For `CultureName`, type the locale where the time stamp is logged. If `CultureName` is blank, it defaults to the same locale currently used by your Windows instance. For more information about supported values, see the `Language tag` column in the table in the Product Behavior topic on MSDN. **Note**
The `div`, `div-MV`, `hu`, and `hu-HU` values are not supported.

7. (Optional) For `TimeZoneKind`, type `Local` or `UTC`. You can set this to provide time zone information when no time zone information is included in your log's time stamp. If this parameter is left blank and if your time stamp doesn't include time zone information, CloudWatch Logs defaults to the local time zone. This parameter is ignored if your time stamp already contains time zone information.

8. (Optional) For `LineCount`, type the number of lines in the header to identify the log file. For example, IIS log files have virtually identical headers. You could enter **5**, which would read the first three lines of the log file header to identify it. In IIS log files, the third line is the date and time stamp, but the time stamp is not always guaranteed to be different between log files. For this reason, we recommend including at least one line of actual log data to uniquely fingerprint the log file.

To send IIS log data to CloudWatch Logs

1. In the JSON file, locate the `IISLog` section.

```
 1 {
 2     "Id": "IISLogs",
 3     "FullName": "AWS.EC2.Windows.CloudWatch.CustomLog.CustomLogInputComponent,AWS.EC2.
           Windows.CloudWatch",
 4     "Parameters": {
 5         "LogDirectoryPath": "C:\\inetpub\\logs\\LogFiles\\W3SVC1",
 6         "TimestampFormat": "yyyy-MM-dd HH:mm:ss",
 7         "Encoding": "UTF-8",
 8         "Filter": "",
 9         "CultureName": "en-US",
10         "TimeZoneKind": "UTC",
11         "LineCount": "5"
12     }
13 },
```

2. For `LogDirectoryPath`, type the folder where IIS logs are stored for an individual site (for example, `C:\inetpub\logs\LogFiles\W3SVCn`). **Note**
Only W3C log format is supported. IIS, NCSA, and Custom formats are not supported.

3. For `TimestampFormat`, type the time stamp format to use. For more information about supported values, see the Custom Date and Time Format Strings topic on MSDN.

4. For `Encoding`, type the file encoding to use (for example, UTF-8). For more information about supported values, see the Encoding Class topic on MSDN. **Note**
Use the encoding name, not the display name.

5. (Optional) For `Filter`, type the prefix of log names. Leave this parameter blank to monitor all files. For more information about supported values, see the FileSystemWatcherFilter Property topic on MSDN.

6. (Optional) For `CultureName`, type the locale where the time stamp is logged. If `CultureName` is blank, it defaults to the same locale currently used by your Windows instance. For more information about supported values, see the **Language tag** column in the table in the Product Behavior topic on MSDN. **Note**
The `div`, `div-MV`, `hu`, and `hu-HU` values are not supported.

7. (Optional) For `TimeZoneKind`, enter `Local` or `UTC`. You can set this to provide time zone information when no time zone information is included in your log's time stamp. If this parameter is left blank and if your time stamp doesn't include time zone information, CloudWatch Logs defaults to the local time zone. This parameter is ignored if your time stamp already contains time zone information.

8. (Optional) For `LineCount`, type the number of lines in the header to identify the log file. For example, IIS log files have virtually identical headers. You could enter **5**, which would read the first five lines of the log file's header to identify it. In IIS log files, the third line is the date and time stamp, but the time stamp is not always guaranteed to be different between log files. For this reason, we recommend including at least one line of actual log data for uniquely fingerprinting the log file.

Step 4: Configure Flow Control

Each data type must have a corresponding destination in the `Flows` section. For example, to send the custom log, ETW log, and system log to CloudWatch Logs, add `(CustomLogs,ETW,SystemEventLog),CloudWatchLogs` to the `Flows` section.

Warning

Adding a step that is not valid blocks the flow. For example, if you add a disk metric step, but your instance doesn't have a disk, all steps in the flow are blocked.

You can send the same log file to more than one destination. For example, to send the application log to two different destinations that you defined in the `CloudWatchLogs` section, add `ApplicationEventLog,(CloudWatchLogs,CloudWatchLogs2)` to the `Flows` section.

To configure flow control

1. In the `AWS.EC2.Windows.CloudWatch.json` file, locate the `Flows` section.

```
1 "Flows": {
2    "Flows": [
3      "PerformanceCounter,CloudWatch",
4      "(PerformanceCounter,PerformanceCounter2), CloudWatch2",
5      "(CustomLogs, ETW, SystemEventLog),CloudWatchLogs",
6      "CustomLogs, CloudWatchLogs2",
7      "ApplicationEventLog,(CloudWatchLogs, CloudWatchLogs2)"
8    ]
9 }
```

2. For `Flows`, add each data type that is to be uploaded (for example, `ApplicationEventLog`) and its destination (for example, `CloudWatchLogs`).

You are now finished editing the JSON file. You use it in a later step.

Start the Agent

To enable an Amazon EC2 instance running Windows Server 2012 or Windows Server 2008 to send logs to CloudWatch Logs, use the EC2Config service (`EC2Config.exe`). Your instance should have EC2Config 4.0 or later, and you can use this procedure. For more information about using an earlier version of EC2Config, see Use EC2Config 3.x or Earlier to Configure CloudWatch in the *Amazon EC2 User Guide for Windows Instances*

To configure CloudWatch using EC2Config 4.x

1. Check the encoding of the AWS.EC2.Windows.CloudWatch.json file that you edited earlier in this procedure. Only UTF-8 without BOM encoding is supported. Then save the file in the following folder on your Windows Server 2008 - 2012 R2 instance: `C:\Program Files\Amazon\SSM\Plugins\awsCloudWatch\`.

2. Start or restart the SSM agent (`AmazonSSMAgent.exe`) using the Windows Services control panel or using the following PowerShell command:

```
1 PS C:\> Restart-Service AmazonSSMAgent
```

After the SSM agent restarts, it detects the configuration file and configures the instance for CloudWatch integration. If you change parameters and settings in the local configuration file, you need to restart the SSM agent to pick up the changes. To disable CloudWatch integration on the instance, change `IsEnabled` to `false` and save your changes in the configuration file.

Report the CloudWatch Logs Agent Status

Use the following procedure to report the status of the CloudWatch Logs agent on your EC2 instance.

To report the agent status

1. Connect to your EC2 instance. For more information, see Connect to Your Instance in the *Amazon EC2 User Guide for Linux Instances.*

   For more information about connection issues, see Troubleshooting Connecting to Your Instance in the *Amazon EC2 User Guide for Linux Instances*

2. At a command prompt, type the following command:

```
1 sudo service awslogs status
```

   If you are running Amazon Linux 2, type the following command:

```
1 sudo service awslogsd status
```

3. Check the **/var/log/awslogs.log** file for any errors, warnings, or issues with the CloudWatch Logs agent.

Start the CloudWatch Logs Agent

If the CloudWatch Logs agent on your EC2 instance did not start automatically after installation, or if you stopped the agent, you can use the following procedure to start the agent.

To start the agent

1. Connect to your EC2 instance. For more information, see Connect to Your Instance in the *Amazon EC2 User Guide for Linux Instances*.

   For more information about connection issues, see Troubleshooting Connecting to Your Instance in the *Amazon EC2 User Guide for Linux Instances*.

2. At a command prompt, type the following command:

```
1 sudo service awslogs start
```

   If you are running Amazon Linux 2, type the following command:

```
1 sudo service awslogsd start
```

Stop the CloudWatch Logs Agent

Use the following procedure to stop the CloudWatch Logs agent on your EC2 instance.

To stop the agent

1. Connect to your EC2 instance. For more information, see Connect to Your Instance in the *Amazon EC2 User Guide for Linux Instances.*

   For more information about connection issues, see Troubleshooting Connecting to Your Instance in the *Amazon EC2 User Guide for Linux Instances.*

2. At a command prompt, type the following command:

```
1 sudo service awslogs stop
```

   If you are running Amazon Linux 2, type the following command:

```
1 sudo service awslogsd stop
```

Quick Start: Use AWS CloudFormation to Get Started With Cloud-Watch Logs

AWS CloudFormation enables you to describe and provision your AWS resources in JSON format. The advantages of this method include being able to manage a collection of AWS resources as a single unit, and easily replicating your AWS resources across regions.

When you provision AWS using AWS CloudFormation, you create templates that describe the AWS resources to use. The following example is a template snippet that creates a log group and a metric filter that counts 404 occurrences and sends this count to the log group.

```
1   "WebServerLogGroup": {
2       "Type": "AWS::Logs::LogGroup",
3       "Properties": {
4           "RetentionInDays": 7
5       }
6   },
7
8   "404MetricFilter": {
9       "Type": "AWS::Logs::MetricFilter",
10      "Properties": {
11          "LogGroupName": {
12              "Ref": "WebServerLogGroup"
13          },
14          "FilterPattern": "[ip, identity, user_id, timestamp, request, status_code = 404, size,
                ...]",
15          "MetricTransformations": [
16              {
17                  "MetricValue": "1",
18                  "MetricNamespace": "test/404s",
19                  "MetricName": "test404Count"
20              }
21          ]
22      }
23  }
```

This is a basic example. You can set up much richer CloudWatch Logs deployments using AWS CloudFormation. For more information about template examples, see Amazon CloudWatch Logs Template Snippets in the *AWS CloudFormation User Guide*. For more information about getting started, see Getting Started with AWS CloudFormation in the *AWS CloudFormation User Guide*.

Working with Log Groups and Log Streams

A log stream is a sequence of log events that share the same source. Each separate source of logs into CloudWatch Logs makes up a separate log stream.

A log group is a group of log streams that share the same retention, monitoring, and access control settings. You can define log groups and specify which streams to put into each group. There is no limit on the number of log streams that can belong to one log group.

Use the procedures in this section to work with log groups and log streams.

Create a Log Group in CloudWatch Logs

When you install the CloudWatch Logs agent on an Amazon EC2 instance using the steps in previous sections of the Amazon CloudWatch Logs User Guide, the log group is created as part of that process. You can also create a log group directly in the CloudWatch console.

To create a log group

1. Open the CloudWatch console at https://console.aws.amazon.com/cloudwatch/.

2. In the navigation pane, choose **Logs**.

3. Choose **Actions**, **Create log group**.

4. Type a name for the log group, and choose **Create log group**.

View Log Data Sent to CloudWatch Logs

You can view and scroll through log data on a stream-by-stream basis as sent to CloudWatch Logs by the CloudWatch Logs agent. You can specify the time range for the log data to view.

To view log data

1. Open the CloudWatch console at https://console.aws.amazon.com/cloudwatch/.

2. In the navigation pane, choose **Logs**.

3. For **Log Groups**, choose the log group to view the streams.

4. For **Log Streams**, choose the log stream name to view the log data.

5. To change how the log data is displayed, do one of the following:

   - To expand all log events, above the list of log events, choose **Expand all**.
   - To expand all log events and view them as plain text, above the list of log events, choose **Text**.
   - To filter the log events, type the desired search filter in the search field. For more information, see Searching and Filtering Log Data.
   - To view log data for a specified date and time range, above the list of log events, choose **custom**. You can choose **Absolute** to specify a date and time range or **Relative** to choose a predefined number of minutes, hours, days, or weeks. You can also switch between **UTC** and **Local timezone**.

Change Log Data Retention in CloudWatch Logs

By default, log data is stored in CloudWatch Logs indefinitely. However, you can configure how long to store log data in a log group. Any data older than the current retention setting is automatically deleted. You can change the log retention for each log group at any time.

To change the logs retention setting

1. Open the CloudWatch console at https://console.aws.amazon.com/cloudwatch/.

2. In the navigation pane, choose **Logs**.

3. Find the log group to update.

4. In the **Expire Events After** column for that log group, choose the current retention setting, such as **Never Expire**.

5. In the **Edit Retention** dialog box, for **Retention**, choose a log retention value, and then choose **Ok**.

Tag Log Groups in Amazon CloudWatch Logs

You can assign your own metadata to the log groups you create in Amazon CloudWatch Logs in the form of *tags*. A tag is a key-value pair that you define for a log group. Using tags is a simple yet powerful way to manage AWS resources and organize data, including billing data.

Topics

- Tag Basics
- Tracking Costs Using Tagging
- Tag Restrictions
- Tagging Log Groups Using the AWS CLI
- Tagging Log Groups Using the CloudWatch Logs API

Tag Basics

You use the AWS CLI or CloudWatch Logs API to complete the following tasks:

- Add tags to a log group when you create it
- Add tags to an existing log group
- List the tags for a log group
- Remove tags from a log group

You can use tags to categorize your log groups. For example, you can categorize them by purpose, owner, or environment. Because you define the key and value for each tag, you can create a custom set of categories to meet your specific needs. For example, you might define a set of tags that helps you track log groups by owner and associated application. Here are several examples of tags:

- Project: Project name
- Owner: Name
- Purpose: Load testing
- Application: Application name
- Environment: Production

Tracking Costs Using Tagging

You can use tags to categorize and track your AWS costs. When you apply tags to your AWS resources, including log groups, your AWS cost allocation report includes usage and costs aggregated by tags. You can apply tags that represent business categories (such as cost centers, application names, or owners) to organize your costs across multiple services. For more information, see Use Cost Allocation Tags for Custom Billing Reports in the *AWS Billing and Cost Management User Guide*.

Tag Restrictions

The following restrictions apply to tags.

Basic restrictions

- The maximum number of tags per log group is 50.
- Tag keys and values are case-sensitive.
- You can't change or edit tags for a deleted log group.

Tag key restrictions

- Each tag key must be unique. If you add a tag with a key that's already in use, your new tag overwrites the existing key-value pair.
- You can't start a tag key with `aws:` because this prefix is reserved for use by AWS. AWS creates tags that begin with this prefix on your behalf, but you can't edit or delete them.
- Tag keys must be between 1 and 128 Unicode characters in length.
- Tag keys must consist of the following characters: Unicode letters, digits, white space, and the following special characters: `_` `.` `/` `=` `+` `-` `@`.

Tag value restrictions

- Tag values must be between 0 and 255 Unicode characters in length.
- Tag values can be blank. Otherwise, they must consist of the following characters: Unicode letters, digits, white space, and any of the following special characters: `_` `.` `/` `=` `+` `-` `@`.

Tagging Log Groups Using the AWS CLI

You can add, list, and remove tags using the AWS CLI. For examples, see the following documentation:

create-log-group
Creates a log group. You can optionally add tags when you create the log group.

tag-log-group
Adds or updates tags for the specified log group.

list-tags-log-group
Lists the tags for the specified log group.

untag-log-group
Removes tags from the specified log group.

Tagging Log Groups Using the CloudWatch Logs API

You can add, list, and remove tags using the CloudWatch Logs API. For examples, see the following documentation:

CreateLogGroup
Creates a log group. You can optionally add tags when you create the log group.

TagLogGroup
Adds or updates tags for the specified log group.

ListTagsLogGroup
Lists the tags for the specified log group.

UntagLogGroup
Removes tags from the specified log group.

Encrypt Log Data in CloudWatch Logs Using AWS KMS

You can encrypt the log data in CloudWatch Logs using an AWS Key Management Service (AWS KMS) customer master key (CMK). Encryption is enabled at the log group level, by associating a CMK with a log group, either when you create the log group or after it exists.

After you associate a CMK with a log group, all newly ingested data for the log group is encrypted using the CMK. This data is stored in encrypted format throughout its retention period. CloudWatch Logs decrypts this data whenever it is requested. CloudWatch Logs must have permissions for the CMK whenever encrypted data is requested.

After you disassociate a CMK from a log group, CloudWatch Logs stops encrypting newly ingested data for the log group. All previously ingested data remains encrypted.

Limits

- To associate a CMK with a log group and perform the following steps, you must have the following permissions: `kms:CreateKey`, `kms:GetKeyPolicy`, and `kms:PutKeyPolicy`.
- After you associate or disassociate a CMK from a log group, it can take up to five minutes for the operation to take effect.
- If you revoke CloudWatch Logs access to an associated CMK or delete an associated CMK, your encrypted data in CloudWatch Logs can no longer be retrieved.
- You cannot associate a CMK with a log group using the CloudWatch console.

Step 1: Create an AWS KMS CMK

To create an AWS KMS CMK, use the following create-key command:

```
1 aws kms create-key
```

The output contains the key ID and Amazon Resource Name (ARN) of the CMK. The following is example output:

```
1  {
2      "KeyMetadata": {
3          "KeyId": "6f815f63-e628-448c-8251-e40cb0d29f59",
4          "Description": "",
5          "Enabled": true,
6          "KeyUsage": "ENCRYPT_DECRYPT",
7          "KeyState": "Enabled",
8          "CreationDate": 1478910250.94,
9          "Arn": "arn:aws:kms:us-west-2:123456789012:key/6f815f63-e628-448c-8251-e40cb0d29f59",
10          "AWSAccountId": "123456789012"
11      }
12  }
```

Step 2: Set Permissions on the CMK

By default, all AWS KMS CMKs are private; only the resource owner can use it to encrypt and decrypt data. However, the resource owner can grant permissions to access the CMK to other users and resources. With this step, you give the CloudWatch service principal permission to use the CMK. This service principal must be in the same region as where the CMK is stored.

First, save the default policy for your CMK as `policy.json` using the following get-key-policy command:

```
1 aws kms get-key-policy --key-id key-id --policy-name default --output text > ./policy.json
```

Open the `policy.json` file in a text editor and add the statement in bold, replacing *region* with the region to use for your log group and separating the existing statement from the new statement with a comma.

```
1  {
2    "Version" : "2012-10-17",
3    "Id" : "key-default-1",
4    "Statement" : [ {
5      "Sid" : "Enable IAM User Permissions",
6      "Effect" : "Allow",
7      "Principal" : {
8        "AWS" : "arn:aws:iam::880185128111:root"
9      },
10     "Action" : "kms:*",
11     "Resource" : "*"
12   },
13   {
14     "Effect": "Allow",
15     "Principal": { "Service": "logs.region.amazonaws.com" },
16     "Action": [
17       "kms:Encrypt*",
18       "kms:Decrypt*",
19       "kms:ReEncrypt*",
20       "kms:GenerateDataKey*",
21       "kms:Describe*"
22     ],
23     "Resource": "*"
24   }
25  ]
26 }
```

Finally, add the updated policy using the following put-key-policy command:

```
1 aws kms put-key-policy --key-id key-id --policy-name default --policy file://policy.json
```

Step 3: Associate a Log Group with a CMK

You can associate a CMK with a log group when you create it or afterwards.

To associate the CMK with a log group when you create it
Use the create-log-group command as follows:

```
1 aws logs create-log-group --log-group-name my-log-group --kms-key-id "key-arn"
```

To associate the CMK with an existing log group
Use the associate-kms-key command as follows:

```
1 aws logs associate-kms-key --log-group-name my-log-group --kms-key-id "key-arn"
```

Step 4: Disassociate a Log Group from a CMK

To disassociate the CMK associated with a log group, use the following disassociate-kms-key command:

```
1 aws logs disassociate-kms-key --log-group-name my-log-group
```

Searching and Filtering Log Data

After the CloudWatch Logs agent begins publishing log data to Amazon CloudWatch, you can begin searching and filtering the log data by creating one or more metric filters. Metric filters define the terms and patterns to look for in log data as it is sent to CloudWatch Logs. CloudWatch Logs uses these metric filters to turn log data into numerical CloudWatch metrics that you can graph or set an alarm on.

Filters do not retroactively filter data. Filters only publish the metric data points for events that happen after the filter was created. Filtered results return the first 50 lines, which will not be displayed if the timestamp on the filtered results is earlier than the metric creation time.

Topics

- Concepts
- Filter and Pattern Syntax
- Creating Metric Filters
- Listing Metric Filters
- Deleting a Metric Filter
- Search Log Data Using Filter Patterns

Concepts

Each metric filter is made up of the following key elements:

filter pattern
A symbolic description of how CloudWatch Logs should interpret the data in each log event. For example, a log entry may contain timestamps, IP addresses, strings, and so on. You use the pattern to specify what to look for in the log file.

metric name
The name of the CloudWatch metric to which the monitored log information should be published. For example, you may publish to a metric called ErrorCount.

metric namespace
The destination namespace of the new CloudWatch metric.

metric value
The numerical value to publish to the metric each time a matching log is found. For example, if you're counting the occurrences of a particular term like "Error", the value will be "1" for each occurrence. If you're counting the bytes transferred, you can increment by the actual number of bytes found in the log event.

default value
The value reported to the metric filter during a period when no matching logs are found. By setting this to 0, you ensure that data is reported during every period, preventing "spotty" metrics with periods of no data.

Filter and Pattern Syntax

You use metric filters to search for and match terms, phrases, or values in your log events. When a metric filter finds one of the terms, phrases, or values in your log events, you can increment the value of a CloudWatch metric. For example, you can create a metric filter to search for and count the occurrence of the word *ERROR* in your log events.

Metric filters can also extract numerical values from space-delimited log events, such as the latency of web requests. In these examples, you can increment your metric value by the actual numerical value extracted from the log.

You can also use conditional operators and wildcards to create exact matches. Before you create a metric filter, you can test your search patterns in the CloudWatch console. The following sections explain the metric filter syntax in more detail.

Matching Terms in Log Events

To search for a term in your log events, use the term as your metric filter pattern. You can specify multiple terms in a metric filter pattern, but all terms must appear in a log event for there to be a match. Metric filters are case sensitive.

Metric filter terms that include characters other than alphanumeric or underscore must be placed inside double quotes ("").

To exclude a term, use a minus sign (-) before the term.

Example 1: Single term
The filter pattern "ERROR" matches log event messages that contain this term, such as the following:

- [ERROR] A fatal exception has occurred
- Exiting with ERRORCODE: -1

Example 2: Include a term and exclude a term
In the previous example, if you change the filter pattern to "ERROR" - "Exiting", the log event message "Exiting with ERRORCODE: -1" would be excluded.

Example 3: Multiple terms
The filter pattern "ERROR Exception" matches log event messages that contain both terms, such as the following:

- [ERROR] Caught IllegalArgumentException
- [ERROR] Unhandled Exception

The filter pattern "Failed to process the request" matches log event messages that contain all terms, such as the following:

- [WARN] Failed to process the request
- [ERROR] Unable to continue: Failed to process the request

OR Pattern Matching

You can match terms in text-based filters using OR pattern matching. For the example patterns below, ERROR (matches ERROR) in pattern 1 and 2. ?ERROR ?WARN (matches lines containing ERROR or WARN) in patterns 1, 2, and 3. ERROR WARN (matches lines containing both ERROR and WARN) in pattern 1. ERROR -WARN (matches lines containing ERROR and not containing WARN) in pattern 2.:

1. ERROR WARN message

2. ERROR message

3. WARN message

You can match terms using OR pattern matching in space-delimited filters. For the example patterns below, [w1=ERROR, w2] matches ERROR (pattern 2), [w1=ERROR || w1=WARN, w2] matches lines containing ERROR or WARN (patterns 2 and 3), [w1=!ERROR&&w1=!WARN, w2] matches lines containing both ERROR and WARN (pattern 1).

1. ERROR WARN message

2. ERROR message

3. WARN message

You can match terms using OR pattern matching in JSON filters. For the example patterns below, {$.foo = bar} matches pattern 1, {$.foo = baz } matches pattern 2, and {$.foo = bar || $.foo = baz } matches pattern 1 and 2.

1. {"foo": "bar"}

2. {"foo": "baz"}

Matching Terms in JSON Log Events

You can extract values from JSON log events. To extract values from JSON log events, you need to create a string-based metric filter. Strings containing scientific notation are not supported. The items in the JSON log event data must exactly match the metric filter. You might want to create metric filters in JSON log events to indicate the following:

- A certain event occurs. For example eventName is "UpdateTrail".
- The IP is outside a known subnet. For example, sourceIPAddress is not in some known subnet range.
- A combination of two or more other conditions are true. For example, the eventName is "UpdateTrail" and the recipientAccountId is 123456789012.

Using Metric Filters to Extract Values from JSON Log Events

You can use metric filters to extract values from JSON log events. A metric filter checks incoming logs and modifies a numeric value when the filter finds a match in the log data. When you create a metric filter, you can simply increment a count each time the matching text is found in a log, or you can extract numerical values from the log and use those to increment the metric value.

Matching JSON Terms Using Metric Filters

The metric filter syntax for JSON log events uses the following format:

```
1  { SELECTOR EQUALITY_OPERATOR STRING }
```

The metric filter must be enclosed in curly braces { }, to indicate this is a JSON expression. The metric filter contains the following parts:

SELECTOR
Specifies what JSON property to check. Property selectors always start with dollar sign ($), which signifies the root of the JSON. Property selectors are alphanumeric strings that also support '-' and '_' characters. Array elements are denoted with [NUMBER] syntax, and must follow a property. Examples are: $.eventId, $.users[0], $.users[0].id, $.requestParameters.instanceId.

EQUALITY_OPERATOR
Can be either = or !=.

STRING
A string with or without quotes. You can use the asterisk '*' wildcard character to match any text at, before, or after a search term. For example, ***Event** will match **PutEvent** and **GetEvent**. **Event*** will match

EventId and **EventName**. **Ev*ent** will only match the actual string **Ev*ent**. Strings that consist entirely of alphanumeric characters do not need to be quoted. Strings that have unicode and other characters such as '@,' '$,' '\,' etc. must be enclosed in double quotes to be valid.

JSON Metric Filter Examples

The following is a JSON example:

```
1  {
2    "eventType": "UpdateTrail",
3    "sourceIPAddress": "111.111.111.111",
4    "arrayKey": [
5        "value",
6        "another value"
7    ],
8    "objectList": [
9        {
10          "name": "a",
11          "id": 1
12       },
13       {
14          "name": "b",
15          "id": 2
16       }
17    ],
18    "SomeObject": null,
19    "ThisFlag": true
20 }
```

The following filters would match:

```
1  { $.eventType = "UpdateTrail" }
```

Filter on the event type being UpdateTrail.

```
1  { $.sourceIPAddress != 123.123.* }
```

Filter on the IP address being outside the subnet 123.123 prefix.

```
1  { $.arrayKey[0] = "value" }
```

Filter on the first entry in arrayKey being "value". If arrayKey is not an array this will be false.

```
1  { $.objectList[1].id = 2 }
```

Filter on the second entry in objectList having a property called id = 2. If objectList is not an array this will be false. If the items in objectList are not objects or do not have an id property, this will be false.

```
1  { $.SomeObject IS NULL }
```

Filter on SomeObject being set to null. This will only be true is the specified object is set to null.

```
1  { $.SomeOtherObject NOT EXISTS }
```

Filter on SomeOtherObject being non-existent. This will only be true if specified object does not exist in log data.

```
1  { $.ThisFlag IS TRUE }
```

Filters on ThisFlag being TRUE. This also works for boolean filters which check for FALSE value.

JSON Compound Conditions

You can combine multiple conditions into a compound expression using OR (||) and AND (&&). Parenthesis are allowed and the syntax follows standard order of operations () > && > ||.

```
1  {
2      "user": {
3          "id": 1,
4          "email": "John.Stiles@example.com"
5      },
6      "users": [
7          {
8              "id": 2,
9              "email": "John.Doe@example.com"
10         },
11         {
12             "id": 3,
13             "email": "Jane.Doe@example.com"
14         }
15     ],
16     "actions": [
17         "GET",
18         "PUT",
19         "DELETE"
20     ],
21     "coordinates": [
22         [0, 1, 2],
23         [4, 5, 6],
24         [7, 8, 9]
25     ]
26 }
```

Examples

```
1  { ($.user.id = 1) && ($.users[0].email = "John.Doe@example.com") }
```

Matches the JSON above.

```
1  { ($.user.id = 2 && $.users[0].email = "nonmatch") || $.actions[2] = "GET" }
```

Doesn't match the JSON above.

```
1  { $.user.email = "John.Stiles@example.com" || $.coordinates[0][1] = nonmatch && $.actions[2] =
      nomatch }
```

Matches the JSON above.

```
1  { ($.user.email = "John.Stiles@example.com" || $.coordinates[0][1] = nonmatch) && $.actions[2] =
      nomatch }
```

Doesn't match the JSON above.

JSON Special Considerations

The SELECTOR must point to a value node (string or number) in the JSON. If it points to an array or object, the filter will not be applied because the log format doesn't match the filter. For example, both {$.users = 1} and {$.users != 1} will fail to match a log event where users is an array:

52

```
1 {
2   "users": [1, 2, 3]
3 }
```

Numeric Comparisons

The metric filter syntax supports precise matching on numeric comparisons. The following numeric comparisons are supported: <, >, >=, <=, =, !=

Numeric filters have a syntax of

```
1 { SELECTOR NUMERIC_OPERATOR NUMBER }
```

The metric filter must be enclosed in curly braces { }, to indicate this is a JSON expression. The metric filter contains the following parts:

SELECTOR

Specifies what JSON property to check. Property selectors always start with dollar sign ($), which signifies the root of the JSON. Property selectors are alphanumeric strings that also support '-' and '_' characters. Array elements are denoted with [NUMBER] syntax, and must follow a property. Examples are: $.latency, $.numbers[0], $.errorCode, $.processes[4].averageRuntime.

NUMERIC_OPERATOR

Can be one of the following: =, !=, <, >, <=, or >=.

NUMBER

An integer with an optional + or - sign, a decimal with an optional + or - sign, or a number in scientific notation, which is an integer or a decimal with an optional + or - sign, followed by 'e', followed by an integer with an optional + or - sign.

Examples:

```
1 { $.latency >= 500 }
2 { $.numbers[0] < 10e3 }
3 { $.numbers[0] < 10e-3 }
4 { $.processes[4].averageRuntime <= 55.5 }
5 { $.errorCode = 400 }
6 { $.errorCode != 500 }
7 { $.latency > +1000 }
```

Using Metric Filters to Extract Values from Space-Delimited Log Events

You can use metric filters to extract values from space-delimited log events. The characters between a pair of square brackets [] or two double quotes ("") are treated as a single field. For example:

```
1 127.0.0.1 - frank [10/Oct/2000:13:25:15 -0700] "GET /apache_pb.gif HTTP/1.0" 200 1534
2 127.0.0.1 - frank [10/Oct/2000:13:35:22 -0700] "GET /apache_pb.gif HTTP/1.0" 500 5324
3 127.0.0.1 - frank [10/Oct/2000:13:50:35 -0700] "GET /apache_pb.gif HTTP/1.0" 200 4355
```

To specify a metric filter pattern that parses space-delimited events, the metric filter pattern has to specify the fields with a name, separated by commas, with the entire pattern enclosed in square brackets. For example: [ip, user, username, timestamp, request, status_code, bytes].

In cases where you don't know the number of fields, you can use shorthand notification using an ellipsis (...). For example:

```
1 [..., status_code, bytes]
2 [ip, user, ..., status_code, bytes]
3 [ip, user, ...]
```

You can also add conditions to your fields so that only log events that match all conditions would match the filters. For example:

```
1  [ip, user, username, timestamp, request, status_code, bytes > 1000]
2  [ip, user, username, timestamp, request, status_code = 200, bytes]
3  [ip, user, username, timestamp, request, status_code = 4*, bytes]
4  [ip, user, username, timestamp, request = *html*, status_code = 4*, bytes]
```

You can use && as an AND operator, as in the following examples:

```
1  [ip, user, username, timestamp, request, status_code = 4* && status_code = 5*, bytes]
2  [ip, user, username, timestamp, request, status_code = 4* && status_code != 403, bytes]
```

CloudWatch Logs supports both string and numeric conditional fields. For string fields, you can use = or != operators with an asterisk (*).

For numeric fields, you can use the $>$, $<$, $>=$, $<=$, $=$, and $!=$ operators.

If you are using a space-delimited filter, extracted fields map to the names of the space-delimited fields (as expressed in the filter) to the value of each of these fields. If you are not using a space-delimited filter, this will be empty.

Example Filter:

```
1  [..., request=*.html*, status_code=4*,]
```

Example log event for the filter:

```
1  127.0.0.1 - frank [10/Oct/2000:13:25:15 -0700] \"GET /index.html HTTP/1.0\" 404 1534
```

Extracted fields for the log event and filter pattern:

```
1  {
2      "$status_code": "404",
3      "$request": "GET /products/index.html HTTP/1.0",
4      "$7": "1534",
5      "$4": "10/Oct/2000:13:25:15 -0700",
6      "$3": "frank",
7      "$2": "-",
8      "$1": "127.0.0.1"
9  }
```

Setting How the Metric Value Changes When Matches Are Found

When a metric filter finds one of the matching terms, phrases, or values in your log events, it increments the count in the CloudWatch metric by the amount you specify for Metric Value. The metric value is aggregated and reported every minute.

If logs are ingested during a one-minute time period but no matches are found, the value specified for Default Value (if any) is reported. However, if no log events are ingested during a one-minute period, then no value is reported.

Specifying a Default Value, even if that value is 0, helps ensure that data is reported more often, helping prevent spotty metrics when matches are not found.

For example, suppose there is a log group that publishes two records every minute and the Metric Value is 1 and the Default Value is 0. If matches are found in the both log records in the first minute, the metric value for that minute is 2. If there are no matches in the log records published in the second minute, the Default Value of 0 is used for both log records and the metric value for that minute is 0.

If you don't specify a Default Value, then no data is reported for any periods where no pattern matches are found.

Publishing Numerical Values Found in Log Entries

Instead of just counting the number of matching items found in logs, you can also use the metric filter to publish values based on numerical values found in the logs. The following procedure shows how to publish a metric with the latency found in the JSON request `metricFilter: { $.latency = * } metricValue: $.latency`.

To publish a metric with the latency in a JSON request

1. Open the CloudWatch console at https://console.aws.amazon.com/cloudwatch/.

2. In the navigation pane, choose **Logs**.

3. In the contents pane, select a log group, and then choose **Create Metric Filter**.

4. On the **Define Logs Metric Filter** screen, for **Filter Pattern**, type **{ $.latency = * }**, and then choose **Assign Metric**.

5. On the **Create Metric Filter and Assign a Metric** screen, choose **Show advanced metric settings**.

6. For **Metric Name**, type **myMetric**.

7. For **Metric Value**, enter **$.latency**.

8. For **Default Value** type 0, and then choose **Create Filter**. Specifying a default value ensures that data is reported even during periods when no log events occur, preventing spotty metrics where data sometimes does not exist.

The following log event would publish a value of 50 to the metric **myMetric** following filter creation.

```
1 {
2 "latency": 50,
3 "requestType": "GET"
4 }
```

Creating Metric Filters

The following examples show how to create metric filters.

Topics

- Example: Count Log Events
- Example: Count Occurrences of a Term
- Example: Count HTTP 404 Codes
- Example: Count HTTP 4xx Codes
- Example: Extract Fields from an Apache Log

Example: Count Log Events

The simplest type of log event monitoring is to count the number of log events that occur. You might want to do this to keep a count of all events, to create a "heartbeat" style monitor or just to practice creating metric filters.

In the following CLI example, a metric filter called MyAppAccessCount is applied to the log group MyApp/access.log to create the metric EventCount in the CloudWatch namespace MyNamespace. The filter is configured to match any log event content and to increment the metric by "1".

To create a metric filter using the CloudWatch console

1. Open the CloudWatch console at https://console.aws.amazon.com/cloudwatch/.

2. In the navigation pane, choose **Logs**.

3. In the contents pane, select a log group, and then choose **Create Metric Filter**.

4. On the **Define Logs Metric Filter** screen, leave **Filter Pattern** blank.

5. Choose **Assign Metric**, and then on the **Create Metric Filter and Assign a Metric** screen, for **Filter Name**, type **EventCount**.

6. Under **Metric Details**, for **Metric Namespace**, type **MyNameSpace**.

7. For **Metric Name**, type **MyAppEventCount**.

8. Choose **Show advanced metric settings** and confirm that **Metric Value** is 1. This specifies that the count is incremented by 1 for every log event.

9. For **Default Value** type 0, and then choose **Create Filter**. Specifying a default value ensures that data is reported even during periods when no log events occur, preventing spotty metrics where data sometimes does not exist.

To create a metric filter using the AWS CLI
At a command prompt, run the following command:

```
1 aws logs put-metric-filter \
2   --log-group-name MyApp/access.log \
3   --filter-name EventCount \
4   --filter-pattern "" \
5   --metric-transformations \
6   metricName=MyAppEventCount,metricNamespace=MyNamespace,metricValue=1,defaultValue=0
```

You can test this new policy by posting any event data. You should see data points published to the metric MyAppAccessEventCount.

To post event data using the AWS CLI
At a command prompt, run the following command:

```
1 aws logs put-log-events \
2   --log-group-name MyApp/access.log --log-stream-name TestStream1 \
3   --log-events \
4     timestamp=1394793518000,message="Test event 1" \
5     timestamp=1394793518000,message="Test event 2" \
6     timestamp=1394793528000,message="This message also contains an Error"
```

Example: Count Occurrences of a Term

Log events frequently include important messages that you want to count, maybe about the success or failure of operations. For example, an error may occur and be recorded to a log file if a given operation fails. You may want to monitor these entries to understand the trend of your errors.

In the example below, a metric filter is created to monitor for the term Error. The policy has been created and added to the log group MyApp/message.log. CloudWatch Logs publishes a data point to the CloudWatch custom metric ErrorCount in the MyApp/message.log namespace with a value of "1" for every event containing Error. If no event contains the word Error, then a value of 0 is published. When graphing this data in the CloudWatch console, be sure to use the sum statistic.

To create a metric filter using the CloudWatch console

1. Open the CloudWatch console at https://console.aws.amazon.com/cloudwatch/.

2. In the navigation pane, choose **Logs**.

3. In the contents pane, select a log group, and then choose **Create Metric Filter**.

4. On the **Define Logs Metric Filter** screen, for **Filter Pattern**, type **Error**. **Note** All entries in **Filter Pattern** are case-sensitive.

5. To test your filter pattern, for **Select Log Data to Test**, select the log group to test the metric filter against, and then choose **Test Pattern**.

6. Under **Results**, CloudWatch Logs displays a message showing how many occurrences of the filter pattern were found in the log file.

   To see detailed results, choose **Show test results**.

7. Choose **Assign Metric**, and then on the **Create Metric Filter and Assign a Metric** screen, for **Filter Name**, type **MyAppErrorCount**.

8. Under **Metric Details**, for **Metric Namespace**, type **MyNameSpace**.

9. For **Metric Name**, type **ErrorCount**.

10. Choose **Show advanced metric settings** and confirm that **Metric Value** is 1. This specifies that the count is incremented by 1 for every log event containing "Error".

11. For **Default Value** type 0, and then choose **Create Filter**.

To create a metric filter using the AWS CLI
At a command prompt, run the following command:

```
1  aws logs put-metric-filter \
2    --log-group-name MyApp/message.log \
3    --filter-name MyAppErrorCount \
4    --filter-pattern 'Error' \
5    --metric-transformations \
6       metricName=EventCount,metricNamespace=MyNamespace,metricValue=1,defaultValue=0
```

You can test this new policy by posting events containing the word "Error" in the message.

To post events using the AWS CLI
At a command prompt, run the following command. Note that patterns are case-sensitive.

```
1  aws logs put-log-events \
2    --log-group-name MyApp/access.log --log-stream-name TestStream1 \
3    --log-events \
4      timestamp=1394793518000,message="This message contains an Error" \
5      timestamp=1394793528000,message="This message also contains an Error"
```

Example: Count HTTP 404 Codes

Using CloudWatch Logs, you can monitor how many times your Apache servers return a HTTP 404 response, which is the response code for page not found. You might want to monitor this to understand how often your site visitors do not find the resource they are looking for. Assume that your log records are structured to include the following information for each log event (site visit):

- Requestor IP Address
- RFC 1413 Identity
- Username
- Timestamp
- Request method with requested resource and protocol
- HTTP response code to request
- Bytes transferred in request

An example of this might look like the following:

```
1 127.0.0.1 - frank [10/Oct/2000:13:55:36 -0700] "GET /apache_pb.gif HTTP/1.0" 404 2326
```

You could specify a rule which attempts to match events of that structure for HTTP 404 errors, as shown in the following example:

To create a metric filter using the CloudWatch console

1. Open the CloudWatch console at https://console.aws.amazon.com/cloudwatch/.

2. In the navigation pane, choose **Logs**.

3. In the contents pane, select a log group, and then choose **Create Metric Filter**.

4. On the **Define Logs Metric Filter** screen, for **Filter Pattern**, type [IP, UserInfo, User, Timestamp, RequestInfo, StatusCode=404, Bytes].

5. To test your filter pattern, for **Select Log Data to Test**, select the log group to test the metric filter against, and then choose **Test Pattern**.

6. Under **Results**, CloudWatch Logs displays a message showing how many occurrences of the filter pattern were found in the log file.

   To see detailed results, choose **Show test results**.

7. Choose **Assign Metric**, and then on the **Create Metric Filter and Assign a Metric** screen, for **Filter Name**, type **HTTP404Errors**.

8. Under **Metric Details**, for **Metric Namespace**, type **MyNameSpace**.

9. For **Metric Name**, type **ApacheNotFoundErrorCount**.

10. Choose **Show advanced metric settings** and confirm that **Metric Value** is 1. This specifies that the count is incremented by 1 for every 404 Error event.

11. For **Default Value** type 0, and then choose **Create Filter**.

To create a metric filter using the AWS CLI
At a command prompt, run the following command:

```
1 aws logs put-metric-filter \
2   --log-group-name MyApp/access.log \
3   --filter-name HTTP404Errors \
4   --filter-pattern '[ip, id, user, timestamp, request, status_code=404, size]' \
5   --metric-transformations \
6       metricName=ApacheNotFoundErrorCount,metricNamespace=MyNamespace,metricValue=1
```

In this example, literal characters such as the left and right square brackets, double quotes and character string 404 were used. The pattern needs to match with the entire log event message for the log event to be considered for monitoring.

You can verify the creation of the metric filter by using the describe-metric-filters command. You should see output that looks like this:

```
1  aws logs describe-metric-filters --log-group-name MyApp/access.log
2
3  {
4      "metricFilters": [
5          {
6              "filterName": "HTTP404Errors",
7              "metricTransformations": [
8                  {
9                      "metricValue": "1",
10                     "metricNamespace": "MyNamespace",
11                     "metricName": "ApacheNotFoundErrorCount"
12                 }
13             ],
14             "creationTime": 1399277571078,
15             "filterPattern": "[ip, id, user, timestamp, request, status_code=404, size]"
16         }
17     ]
18 }
```

Now you can post a few events manually:

```
1  aws logs put-log-events \
2  --log-group-name MyApp/access.log --log-stream-name hostname \
3  --log-events \
4  timestamp=1394793518000,message="127.0.0.1 - bob [10/Oct/2000:13:55:36 -0700] \"GET /apache_pb.
       gif HTTP/1.0\" 404 2326" \
5  timestamp=1394793528000,message="127.0.0.1 - bob [10/Oct/2000:13:55:36 -0700] \"GET /apache_pb2.
       gif HTTP/1.0\" 200 2326"
```

Soon after putting these sample log events, you can retrieve the metric named in the CloudWatch console as ApacheNotFoundErrorCount.

Example: Count HTTP 4xx Codes

As in the previous example, you might want to monitor your web service access logs and monitor the HTTP response code levels. For example, you might want to monitor all of the HTTP 400-level errors. However, you might not want to specify a new metric filter for every return code.

The following example demonstrates how to create a metric that includes all 400-level HTTP code responses from an access log using the Apache access log format from the Example: Count HTTP 404 Codes example.

To create a metric filter using the CloudWatch console

1. Open the CloudWatch console at https://console.aws.amazon.com/cloudwatch/.

2. In the navigation pane, choose **Logs**.

3. In the contents pane, select a log group, and then choose **Create Metric Filter**.

4. On the **Define Logs Metric Filter** screen, for **Filter Pattern**, type [**ip, id, user, timestamp, request, status_code=4*, size**].

5. To test your filter pattern, for **Select Log Data to Test**, select the log group to test the metric filter against, and then choose **Test Pattern**.

6. Under **Results**, CloudWatch Logs displays a message showing how many occurrences of the filter pattern were found in the log file.

   To see detailed results, click **Show test results**.

7. Choose **Assign Metric**, and then on the **Create Metric Filter and Assign a Metric** screen, for **Filter Name**, type **HTTP4xxErrors**.

8. Under **Metric Details**, for **Metric Namespace**, type **MyNameSpace**.

9. For **Metric Name**, type **HTTP4xxErrors**.

10. Choose **Show advanced metric settings** and confirm that **Metric Value** is 1. This specifies that the count is incremented by 1 for every log containing a 4xx error.

11. For **Default Value** type 0, and then choose **Create Filter**.

To create a metric filter using the AWS CLI
At a command prompt, run the following command:

```
1 aws logs put-metric-filter \
2   --log-group-name MyApp/access.log \
3   --filter-name HTTP4xxErrors \
4   --filter-pattern '[ip, id, user, timestamp, request, status_code=4*, size]' \
5   --metric-transformations \
6   metricName=HTTP4xxErrors,metricNamespace=MyNamespace,metricValue=1,defaultValue=0
```

You can use the following data in put-event calls to test this rule. If you did not remove the monitoring rule in the previous example, you will generate two different metrics.

```
1 127.0.0.1 - - [24/Sep/2013:11:49:52 -0700] "GET /index.html HTTP/1.1" 404 287
2 127.0.0.1 - - [24/Sep/2013:11:49:52 -0700] "GET /index.html HTTP/1.1" 404 287
3 127.0.0.1 - - [24/Sep/2013:11:50:51 -0700] "GET /~test/ HTTP/1.1" 200 3
4 127.0.0.1 - - [24/Sep/2013:11:50:51 -0700] "GET /favicon.ico HTTP/1.1" 404 308
5 127.0.0.1 - - [24/Sep/2013:11:50:51 -0700] "GET /favicon.ico HTTP/1.1" 404 308
6 127.0.0.1 - - [24/Sep/2013:11:51:34 -0700] "GET /~test/index.html HTTP/1.1" 200 3
```

Example: Extract Fields from an Apache Log

Sometimes, instead of counting, it is helpful to use values within individual log events for metric values. This example shows how you can create an extraction rule to create a metric that measures the bytes transferred by an Apache webserver.

This extraction rule matches the seven fields of the log event. The metric value is the value of the seventh matched token. You can see the reference to the token as "$7" in the `metricValue` field of the extraction rule.

To create a metric filter using the CloudWatch console

1. Open the CloudWatch console at https://console.aws.amazon.com/cloudwatch/.

2. In the navigation pane, choose **Logs**.

3. In the contents pane, select a log group, and then choose **Create Metric Filter**.

4. On the **Define Logs Metric Filter** screen, for **Filter Pattern**, type [**ip, id, user, timestamp, request, status_code, size**].

5. To test your filter pattern, for **Select Log Data to Test**, select the log group to test the metric filter against, and then choose **Test Pattern**.

6. Under **Results**, CloudWatch Logs displays a message showing how many occurrences of the filter pattern were found in the log file.

   To see detailed results, click **Show test results**.

7. Choose **Assign Metric**, and then on the **Create Metric Filter and Assign a Metric** screen, for **Filter Name**, type **size**.

8. Under **Metric Details**, for **Metric Namespace**, type **MyNameSpace**.

9. For **Metric Name**, type **BytesTransferred**

10. Choose **Show advanced metric settings** and for **Metric Value** type **$size**.

11. For **Default Value** type 0, and then choose **Create Filter**.

To create a metric filter using the AWS CLI
At a command prompt, run the following command

```
1 aws logs put-metric-filter \
2 --log-group-name MyApp/access.log \
3 --filter-name BytesTransferred \
4 --filter-pattern '[ip, id, user, timestamp, request, status_code=4*, size]' \
5 --metric-transformations \
6 metricName=BytesTransferred,metricNamespace=MyNamespace,metricValue=$size,defaultValue=0
```

You can use the following data in put-log-event calls to test this rule. This generates two different metrics if you did not remove monitoring rule in the previous example.

```
1 127.0.0.1 - - [24/Sep/2013:11:49:52 -0700] "GET /index.html HTTP/1.1" 404 287
2 127.0.0.1 - - [24/Sep/2013:11:49:52 -0700] "GET /index.html HTTP/1.1" 404 287
3 127.0.0.1 - - [24/Sep/2013:11:50:51 -0700] "GET /~test/ HTTP/1.1" 200 3
4 127.0.0.1 - - [24/Sep/2013:11:50:51 -0700] "GET /favicon.ico HTTP/1.1" 404 308
5 127.0.0.1 - - [24/Sep/2013:11:50:51 -0700] "GET /favicon.ico HTTP/1.1" 404 308
6 127.0.0.1 - - [24/Sep/2013:11:51:34 -0700] "GET /~test/index.html HTTP/1.1" 200 3
```

Listing Metric Filters

You can list all metric filters in a log group.

To list metric filters using the CloudWatch console

1. Open the CloudWatch console at https://console.aws.amazon.com/cloudwatch/.

2. In the navigation pane, choose **Logs**.

3. In the contents pane, in the list of log groups, in the **Metric Filters** column, choose the number of filters.

    The **Log Groups > Filters for** screen lists all metric filters associated with the log group.

To list metric filters using the AWS CLI
At a command prompt, run the following command:

```
1 aws logs describe-metric-filters --log-group-name MyApp/access.log
```

The following is example output:

```
1  {
2      "metricFilters": [
3          {
4              "filterName": "HTTP404Errors",
5              "metricTransformations": [
6                  {
7                      "metricValue": "1",
8                      "metricNamespace": "MyNamespace",
9                      "metricName": "ApacheNotFoundErrorCount"
10                 }
11             ],
12             "creationTime": 1399277571078,
13             "filterPattern": "[ip, id, user, timestamp, request, status_code=404, size]"
14         }
15     ]
16 }
```

Deleting a Metric Filter

A policy is identified by its name and the log group it belongs to.

To delete a metric filter using the CloudWatch console

1. Open the CloudWatch console at https://console.aws.amazon.com/cloudwatch/.

2. In the navigation pane, choose **Logs**.

3. In the contents pane, in the **Metric Filter** column, choose the metric filter.

4. On the **Logs Metric Filters** screen, in the metric filter, choose **Delete Filter**.

5. When prompted for confirmation, choose **Yes, Delete**.

To delete a metric filter using the AWS CLI

At a command prompt, run the following command:

```
1 aws logs delete-metric-filter --log-group-name MyApp/access.log \
2   --filter-name MyFilterName
```

Search Log Data Using Filter Patterns

You can search your log data using the Filter and Pattern Syntax. You can search all the log streams within a log group, or by using the AWS CLI you can also search specific log streams. When each search runs, it returns up to the first page of data found and a token to retrieve the next page of data or to continue searching. If no results are returned, you can continue searching.

You can set the time range you want to query to limit the scope of your search. You could start with a larger range to see where the log lines you are interested in fall, and then shorten the time range to scope the view to logs in the time range that interest you.

You can also pivot directly from your logs-extracted metrics to the corresponding logs.

Search Log Entries Using the Console

You can search for log entries that meet a specified criteria using the console.

To search your logs using the console

1. Open the CloudWatch console at https://console.aws.amazon.com/cloudwatch/.

2. In the navigation pane, choose **Logs**.

3. For **Log Groups**, choose the name of the log group containing the log stream to search.

4. For **Log Streams**, choose the name of the log stream to search.

5. For **Filter**, type the metric filter syntax to use and then press Enter.

To search all log entries for a time range using the console

1. Open the CloudWatch console at https://console.aws.amazon.com/cloudwatch/.

2. In the navigation pane, choose **Logs**.

3. For **Log Groups**, choose the name of the log group containing the log stream to search.

4. Choose **Search Events**.

5. For **Filter**, type the metric filter syntax to use, select the date and time range, and then press Enter.

Search Log Entries Using the AWS CLI

You can search for log entries that meet a specified criteria using the AWS CLI.

To search log entries using the AWS CLI
At a command prompt, run the following filter-log-events command. Use `--filter-pattern` to limit the results to the specified filter pattern and `--log-stream-names` to limit the results to the specified log group.

```
1 aws logs filter-log-events --log-group-name my-group [--log-stream-names
      LIST_OF_STREAMS_TO_SEARCH] --filter-pattern VALID_METRIC_FILTER_PATTERN]
```

To search log entries over a given time range using the AWS CLI
At a command prompt, run the following filter-log-events command:

```
1 aws logs filter-log-events --log-group-name my-group [--log-stream-names
      LIST_OF_STREAMS_TO_SEARCH] [--start-time 1482197400000] [--end-time 1482217558365] [--filter
      -pattern VALID_METRIC_FILTER_PATTERN]
```

Pivot from Metrics to Logs

You can get to specific log entries from other parts of the console.

To get from dashboard widgets to logs

1. Open the CloudWatch console at https://console.aws.amazon.com/cloudwatch/.

2. In the navigation pane, choose **Dashboards**.

3. Choose a dashboard.

4. On the widget, choose the **View logs** icon, and then choose **View logs in this time range**. If there is more than one metric filter, select one from the list. If there are more metric filters than we can display in the list, choose **More metric filters** and select or search for a metric filter.

To get from metrics to logs

1. Open the CloudWatch console at https://console.aws.amazon.com/cloudwatch/.

2. In the navigation pane, choose **Metrics**.

3. In the search field on the **All metrics** tab, type the name of the metric and press Enter.

4. Select one or more metrics from the results of your search.

5. Choose **Actions**, **View logs**. If there is more than one metric filter, select one from the list. If there are more metric filters than we can display in the list, choose **More metric filters** and select or search for a metric filter.

Troubleshooting

Search takes too long to complete

If you have a lot of log data, search might take a long time to complete. To speed up a search, you can do the following:

- If you are using the AWS CLI, you can limit the search to just the log streams you are interested in. For example, if your log group has 1000 log streams, but you just want to see three log streams that you know are relevant, you can use the AWS CLI to limit your search to only those three log streams within the log group.
- Use a shorter, more granular time range, which reduces the amount of data to be searched and speeds up the query.

Real-time Processing of Log Data with Subscriptions

You can use subscriptions to get access to a real-time feed of log events from CloudWatch Logs and have it delivered to other services such as an Amazon Kinesis stream, Amazon Kinesis Data Firehose stream, or AWS Lambda for custom processing, analysis, or loading to other systems. To begin subscribing to log events, create the receiving source, such as a Kinesis stream, where the events will be delivered. A subscription filter defines the filter pattern to use for filtering which log events get delivered to your AWS resource, as well as information about where to send matching log events to.

CloudWatch Logs also produces CloudWatch metrics about the forwarding of log events to subscriptions. For more information, see Amazon CloudWatch Logs Metrics and Dimensions.

Topics

- Concepts
- Using CloudWatch Logs Subscription Filters
- Cross-Account Log Data Sharing with Subscriptions

Concepts

Each subscription filter is made up of the following key elements:

log group name
The log group to associate the subscription filter with. All log events uploaded to this log group would be subject to the subscription filter and would be delivered to the chosen Kinesis stream if the filter pattern matches with the log events.

filter pattern
A symbolic description of how CloudWatch Logs should interpret the data in each log event, along with filtering expressions that restrict what gets delivered to the destination AWS resource. For more information about the filter pattern syntax, see Filter and Pattern Syntax.

destination arn
The Amazon Resource Name (ARN) of the Kinesis stream, Kinesis Data Firehose stream, or Lambda function you want to use as the destination of the subscription feed.

role arn
An IAM role that grants CloudWatch Logs the necessary permissions to put data into the chosen Kinesis stream. This role is not needed for Lambda destinations because CloudWatch Logs can get the necessary permissions from access control settings on the Lambda function itself.

distribution
The method used to distribute log data to the destination, when the destination is an Amazon Kinesis stream. By default, log data is grouped by log stream. For a more even distribution, you can group log data randomly.

Using CloudWatch Logs Subscription Filters

You can use a subscription filter with Kinesis, Lambda, or Kinesis Data Firehose.

Topics

- Example 1: Subscription Filters with Kinesis
- Example 2: Subscription Filters with AWS Lambda
- Example 3: Subscription Filters with Amazon Kinesis Data Firehose

Example 1: Subscription Filters with Kinesis

The following example associates a subscription filter with a log group containing AWS CloudTrail events to have every logged activity made by "Root" AWS credentials delivered to an Kinesis stream called "RootAccess." For more information about how to send AWS CloudTrail events to CloudWatch Logs, see Sending CloudTrail Events to CloudWatch Logs in the *AWS CloudTrail User Guide*.

Note
Before you create the Kinesis stream, calculate the volume of log data that will be generated. Be sure to create a Kinesis stream with enough shards to handle this volume. If the stream does not have enough shards, the log stream will be throttled. For more information about Kinesis stream volume limits, see Amazon Kinesis Data Streams Limits.

To create a subscription filter for Kinesis

1. Create a destination Kinesis stream using the following command:

```
$ C:\>  aws kinesis create-stream --stream-name "RootAccess" --shard-count 1
```

2. Wait until the Kinesis stream becomes Active (this might take a minute or two). You can use the following Kinesis describe-stream command to check the **StreamDescription.StreamStatus** property. In addition, note the **StreamDescription.StreamARN** value, as you will need it in a later step:

```
aws kinesis describe-stream --stream-name "RootAccess"
```

The following is example output:

```
{
    "StreamDescription": {
        "StreamStatus": "ACTIVE",
        "StreamName": "RootAccess",
        "StreamARN": "arn:aws:kinesis:us-east-1:123456789012:stream/RootAccess",
        "Shards": [
            {
                "ShardId": "shardId-000000000000",
                "HashKeyRange": {
                    "EndingHashKey": "340282366920938463463374607431768211455",
                    "StartingHashKey": "0"
                },
                "SequenceNumberRange": {
                    "StartingSequenceNumber":
                    "49551135218688818456679503831981458784591352702181572610"
                }
            }
        ]
    }
}
```

3. Create the IAM role that will grant CloudWatch Logs permission to put data into your Kinesis stream. First, you'll need to create a trust policy in a file (for example, ~/TrustPolicyForCWL.json). Use a text editor to create this policy. Do not use the IAM console to create it.

```
{
  "Statement": {
    "Effect": "Allow",
    "Principal": { "Service": "logs.region.amazonaws.com" },
    "Action": "sts:AssumeRole"
  }
}
```

4. Use the **create-role** command to create the IAM role, specifying the trust policy file. Note the returned **Role.Arn** value, as you will also need it for a later step:

```
aws iam create-role --role-name CWLtoKinesisRole --assume-role-policy-document file://~/
    TrustPolicyForCWL.json
```

```
{
    "Role": {
        "AssumeRolePolicyDocument": {
            "Statement": {
                "Action": "sts:AssumeRole",
                "Effect": "Allow",
                "Principal": {
                    "Service": "logs.region.amazonaws.com"
                }
            }
        },
        "RoleId": "AAOIIAH450GAB4HC5F431",
        "CreateDate": "2015-05-29T13:46:29.431Z",
        "RoleName": "CWLtoKinesisRole",
        "Path": "/",
        "Arn": "arn:aws:iam::123456789012:role/CWLtoKinesisRole"
    }
}
```

5. Create a permissions policy to define what actions CloudWatch Logs can do on your account. First, you'll create a permissions policy in a file (for example, ~/PermissionsForCWL.json). Use a text editor to create this policy. Do not use the IAM console to create it.

```
{
  "Statement": [
    {
      "Effect": "Allow",
      "Action": "kinesis:PutRecord",
      "Resource": "arn:aws:kinesis:region:123456789012:stream/RootAccess"
    },
    {
      "Effect": "Allow",
      "Action": "iam:PassRole",
      "Resource": "arn:aws:iam::123456789012:role/CWLtoKinesisRole"
    }
  ]
}
```

6. Associate the permissions policy with the role using the following put-role-policy command:

```
1 aws iam put-role-policy --role-name CWLtoKinesisRole --policy-name Permissions-Policy-For-
      CWL --policy-document file://~/PermissionsForCWL.json
```

7. After the Kinesis stream is in **Active** state and you have created the IAM role, you can create the CloudWatch Logs subscription filter. The subscription filter immediately starts the flow of real-time log data from the chosen log group to your Kinesis stream:

```
1 aws logs put-subscription-filter \
2     --log-group-name "CloudTrail" \
3     --filter-name "RootAccess" \
4     --filter-pattern "{$.userIdentity.type = Root}" \
5     --destination-arn "arn:aws:kinesis:region:123456789012:stream/RootAccess" \
6     --role-arn "arn:aws:iam::123456789012:role/CWLtoKinesisRole"
```

8. After you set up the subscription filter, CloudWatch Logs forwards all the incoming log events that match the filter pattern to your Kinesis stream. You can verify that this is happening by grabbing an Kinesis shard iterator and using the Kinesis get-records command to fetch some Kinesis records:

```
1 aws kinesis get-shard-iterator --stream-name RootAccess --shard-id shardId-000000000000 --
      shard-iterator-type TRIM_HORIZON
```

```
1 {
2     "ShardIterator":
3     "AAAAAAAAAAFGU/
        kLvNggvndHq2UIFOw5PZc6F01s3e3afsSscRM70JSbjIefg2ub07nk1y6CDxYR1UoGHJNP4m4NFUetzfL+
        wev+e2P4djJg4L9wmXKvQYoE+rMUiFq+p4Cn3IgvqOb5dRAOyybNdRcdzvnC35KQANoHzzahKdRGb9v4scv
        +3vaq+f+OIK8zM5My8ID+g6rMo7UKWeI4+IWiK2OShOuP"
4 }
```

```
1 aws kinesis get-records --limit 10 --shard-iterator "AAAAAAAAAAFGU/
      kLvNggvndHq2UIFOw5PZc6F01s3e3afsSscRM70JSbjIefg2ub07nk1y6CDxYR1UoGHJNP4m4NFUetzfL+wev+
      e2P4djJg4L9wmXKvQYoE+rMUiFq+p4Cn3IgvqOb5dRAOyybNdRcdzvnC35KQANoHzzahKdRGb9v4scv+3vaq+f+
      OIK8zM5My8ID+g6rMo7UKWeI4+IWiK2OShOuP"
```

Note that you might need to make this call a few times before Kinesis starts to return data.

You should expect to see a response with an array of records. The **Data** attribute in an Kinesis record is Base64 encoded and compressed with the gzip format. You can examine the raw data from the command line using the following Unix commands:

```
1 echo -n "<Content of Data>" | base64 -d | zcat
```

The Base64 decoded and decompressed data is formatted as JSON with the following structure:

```
1 {
2     "owner": "111111111111",
3     "logGroup": "CloudTrail",
4     "logStream": "111111111111_CloudTrail_us-east-1",
5     "subscriptionFilters": [
6         "Destination"
7     ],
8     "messageType": "DATA_MESSAGE",
9     "logEvents": [
10        {
11            "id": "31953106060696983378809025079804211143289615424298221568",
12            "timestamp": 1432826855000,
```

```
13          "message": "{\"eventVersion\":\"1.03\",\"userIdentity\":{\"type\":\"Root\"}"
14      },
15      {
16          "id": "31953106606096669833788090250798042111432896154242982215691569",
17          "timestamp": 1432826855000,
18          "message": "{\"eventVersion\":\"1.03\",\"userIdentity\":{\"type\":\"Root\"}"
19      },
20      {
21          "id": "31953106606096669833788090250798042111432896154242982215701570",
22          "timestamp": 1432826855000,
23          "message": "{\"eventVersion\":\"1.03\",\"userIdentity\":{\"type\":\"Root\"}"
24      }
25   ]
26 }
```

The key elements in the above data structure are the following:

owner
The AWS Account ID of the originating log data.

logGroup
The log group name of the originating log data.

logStream
The log stream name of the originating log data.

subscriptionFilters
The list of subscription filter names that matched with the originating log data.

messageType
Data messages will use the "DATA_MESSAGE" type. Sometimes CloudWatch Logs may emit Kinesis records with a "CONTROL_MESSAGE" type, mainly for checking if the destination is reachable.

logEvents
The actual log data, represented as an array of log event records. The "id" property is a unique identifier for every log event.

Example 2: Subscription Filters with AWS Lambda

In this example, you'll create a CloudWatch Logs subscription filter that sends log data to your AWS Lambda function.

Note
Before you create the Lambda function, calculate the volume of log data that will be generated. Be sure to create a function that can handle this volume. If the function does not have enough volume, the log stream will be throttled. For more information about Lambda limits, see AWS Lambda Limits.

To create a subscription filter for Lambda

1. Create the AWS Lambda function.

   Ensure that you have set up the Lambda execution role. For more information, see Step 2.2: Create an IAM Role (execution role) in the *AWS Lambda Developer Guide*.

2. Open a text editor and create a file named `helloWorld.js` with the following contents:

```
1 var zlib = require('zlib');
2 exports.handler = function(input, context) {
3     var payload = new Buffer(input.awslogs.data, 'base64');
4     zlib.gunzip(payload, function(e, result) {
5         if (e) {
6             context.fail(e);
7         } else {
```

```
 8                  result = JSON.parse(result.toString('ascii'));
 9                  console.log("Event Data:", JSON.stringify(result, null, 2));
10                  context.succeed();
11              }
12          });
13  };
```

3. Zip the file helloWorld.js and save it with the name `helloWorld.zip`.

4. Use the following command, where the role is the Lambda execution role you set up in the first step:

```
1  aws lambda create-function \
2      --function-name helloworld \
3      --zip-file file://file-path/helloWorld.zip \
4      --role lambda-execution-role-arn \
5      --handler helloWorld.handler \
6      --runtime nodejs4.3
```

5. Grant CloudWatch Logs the permission to execute your function. Use the following command, replacing the placeholder account with your own account and the placeholder log group with the log group to process:

```
1  aws lambda add-permission \
2      --function-name "helloworld" \
3      --statement-id "helloworld" \
4      --principal "logs.region.amazonaws.com" \
5      --action "lambda:InvokeFunction" \
6      --source-arn "arn:aws:logs:region:123456789123:log-group:TestLambda:*" \
7      --source-account "123456789012"
```

6. Create a subscription filter using the following command, replacing the placeholder account with your own account and the placeholder log group with the log group to process:

```
1  aws logs put-subscription-filter \
2      --log-group-name myLogGroup \
3      --filter-name demo \
4      --filter-pattern "" \
5      --destination-arn arn:aws:lambda:region:123456789123:function:helloworld
```

7. (Optional) Test using a sample log event. At a command prompt, run the following command, which will put a simple log message into the subscribed stream.

   To see the output of your Lambda function, navigate to the Lambda function where you will see the output in /aws/lambda/helloworld:

```
1  aws logs put-log-events --log-group-name myLogGroup --log-stream-name stream1 --log-events
       "[{\"timestamp\":<CURRENT TIMESTAMP MILLIS> , \"message\": \"Simple Lambda Test\"}]"
```

   You should expect to see a response with an array of Lambda. The **Data** attribute in the Lambda record is Base64 encoded and compressed with the gzip format. The actual payload that Lambda receives is in the following format { "awslogs": {"data": "BASE64ENCODED_GZIP_COMPRESSED_DATA"} } You can examine the raw data from the command line using the following Unix commands:

```
1  echo -n "<BASE64ENCODED_GZIP_COMPRESSED_DATA>" | base64 -d | zcat
```

   The Base64 decoded and decompressed data is formatted as JSON with the following structure:

```
1  {
2      "owner": "123456789012",
3      "logGroup": "CloudTrail",
```

```
4       "logStream": "123456789012_CloudTrail_us-east-1",
5       "subscriptionFilters": [
6           "Destination"
7       ],
8       "messageType": "DATA_MESSAGE",
9       "logEvents": [
10          {
11              "id": "31953106060696669833788090250798042111432896154242
98221568",
12              "timestamp": 1432826855000,
13              "message": "{\"eventVersion\":\"1.03\",\"userIdentity\":{\"type\":\"Root\"}"
14          },
15          {
16              "id": "31953106060696669833788090250798042111432896154242
98221569",
17              "timestamp": 1432826855000,
18              "message": "{\"eventVersion\":\"1.03\",\"userIdentity\":{\"type\":\"Root\"}"
19          },
20          {
21              "id": "31953106060696669833788090250798042111432896154242
98221570",
22              "timestamp": 1432826855000,
23              "message": "{\"eventVersion\":\"1.03\",\"userIdentity\":{\"type\":\"Root\"}"
24          }
25      ]
26  }
```

The key elements in the above data structure are the following:

owner
The AWS Account ID of the originating log data.

logGroup
The log group name of the originating log data.

logStream
The log stream name of the originating log data.

subscriptionFilters
The list of subscription filter names that matched with the originating log data.

messageType
Data messages will use the "DATA_MESSAGE" type. Sometimes CloudWatch Logs may emit Lambda records with a "CONTROL_MESSAGE" type, mainly for checking if the destination is reachable.

logEvents
The actual log data, represented as an array of log event records. The "id" property is a unique identifier for every log event.

Example 3: Subscription Filters with Amazon Kinesis Data Firehose

In this example, you'll create a CloudWatch Logs subscription that sends any incoming log events that match your defined filters to your Amazon Kinesis Data Firehose delivery stream. Data sent from CloudWatch Logs to Amazon Kinesis Data Firehose is already compressed with gzip level 6 compression, so you do not need to use compression within your Kinesis Data Firehose delivery stream.

Note
Before you create the Kinesis Firehose stream, calculate the volume of log data that will be generated. Be sure to create a Kinesis Firehose stream that can handle this volume. If the stream cannot handle the volume, the log stream will be throttled. For more information about Kinesis Firehose stream volume limits, see Amazon Kinesis Firehose Data Limits.

To create a subscription filter for Kinesis Data Firehose

73

1. Create an Amazon Simple Storage Service (Amazon S3) bucket. We recommend that you use a bucket that was created specifically for CloudWatch Logs. However, if you want to use an existing bucket, skip to step 2.

   Run the following command, replacing the placeholder region with the region you want to use:

```
1 aws s3api create-bucket --bucket my-bucket --create-bucket-configuration LocationConstraint
     =region
```

   The following is example output:

```
1 {
2     "Location": "/my-bucket"
3 }
```

2. Create the IAM role that will grant Amazon Kinesis Data Firehose permission to put data into your Amazon S3 bucket.

   For more information, see Controlling Access with Amazon Kinesis Data Firehose in the *Amazon Kinesis Data Firehose Developer Guide.*

   First, use a text editor to create a trust policy in a file ~/TrustPolicyForFirehose.json as follows, replacing *account-id* with your AWS account ID:

```
1 {
2   "Statement": {
3     "Effect": "Allow",
4     "Principal": { "Service": "firehose.amazonaws.com" },
5     "Action": "sts:AssumeRole",
6     "Condition": { "StringEquals": { "sts:ExternalId":"account-id" } }
7   }
8  }
```

3. Use the **create-role** command to create the IAM role, specifying the trust policy file. Note of the returned **Role.Arn** value, as you will need it in a later step:

```
1 aws iam create-role \
2       --role-name FirehosetoS3Role \
3       --assume-role-policy-document file://~/TrustPolicyForFirehose.json
4
5 {
6     "Role": {
7         "AssumeRolePolicyDocument": {
8             "Statement": {
9                 "Action": "sts:AssumeRole",
10                "Effect": "Allow",
11                "Principal": {
12                    "Service": "logs.region.amazonaws.com"
13                }
14            }
15        },
16        "RoleId": "AAOIIAH450GAB4HC5F431",
17        "CreateDate": "2015-05-29T13:46:29.431Z",
18        "RoleName": "FirehosetoS3Role",
19        "Path": "/",
20        "Arn": "arn:aws:iam::123456789012:role/FirehosetoS3Role"
21    }
22 }
```

4. Create a permissions policy to define what actions Kinesis Data Firehose can do on your account. First, use a text editor to create a permissions policy in a file `~/PermissionsForFirehose.json`:

```
1  {
2    "Statement": [
3      {
4        "Effect": "Allow",
5        "Action": [
6          "s3:AbortMultipartUpload",
7          "s3:GetBucketLocation",
8          "s3:GetObject",
9          "s3:ListBucket",
10         "s3:ListBucketMultipartUploads",
11         "s3:PutObject" ],
12       "Resource": [
13         "arn:aws:s3:::my-bucket",
14         "arn:aws:s3:::my-bucket/*" ]
15     }
16   ]
17 }
```

5. Associate the permissions policy with the role using the following put-role-policy command:

```
1  aws iam put-role-policy --role-name FirehosetoS3Role --policy-name Permissions-Policy-For-
      Firehose --policy-document file://~/PermissionsForFirehose.json
```

6. Create a destination Kinesis Data Firehose delivery stream as follows, replacing the placeholder values for **RoleARN** and **BucketARN** with the role and bucket ARNs that you created:

```
1  aws firehose create-delivery-stream \
2  --delivery-stream-name 'my-delivery-stream' \
3  --s3-destination-configuration \
4  RoleARN='arn:aws:iam::123456789012:role/FirehosetoS3Role',BucketARN='arn:aws:s3:::my-bucket
      '
```

Note that Kinesis Data Firehose automatically uses a prefix in YYYY/MM/DD/HH UTC time format for delivered Amazon S3 objects. You can specify an extra prefix to be added in front of the time format prefix. If the prefix ends with a forward slash (/), it appears as a folder in the Amazon S3 bucket.

7. Wait until the stream becomes active (this might take a few minutes). You can use the Kinesis Data Firehose **describe-delivery-stream** command to check the **DeliveryStreamDescription.DeliveryStreamStatus** property. In addition, note the **DeliveryStreamDescription.DeliveryStreamARN** value, as you will need it in a later step:

```
1  aws firehose describe-delivery-stream --delivery-stream-name "my-delivery-stream"
2  {
3      "DeliveryStreamDescription": {
4          "HasMoreDestinations": false,
5          "VersionId": "1",
6          "CreateTimestamp": 1446075815.822,
7          "DeliveryStreamARN": "arn:aws:firehose:us-east-1:123456789012:deliverystream/my-
              delivery-stream",
8          "DeliveryStreamStatus": "ACTIVE",
9          "DeliveryStreamName": "my-delivery-stream",
10         "Destinations": [
11             {
12                 "DestinationId": "destinationId-000000000001",
```

```
13              "S3DestinationDescription": {
14                  "CompressionFormat": "UNCOMPRESSED",
15                  "EncryptionConfiguration": {
16                      "NoEncryptionConfig": "NoEncryption"
17                  },
18                  "RoleARN": "delivery-stream-role",
19                  "BucketARN": "arn:aws:s3:::my-bucket",
20                  "BufferingHints": {
21                      "IntervalInSeconds": 300,
22                      "SizeInMBs": 5
23                  }
24              }
25          }
26      ]
27  }
28  }
```

8. Create the IAM role that will grant CloudWatch Logs permission to put data into your Kinesis Data Firehose delivery stream. First, use a text editor to create a trust policy in a file ~/TrustPolicyForCWL.json:

```
1 {
2   "Statement": {
3     "Effect": "Allow",
4     "Principal": { "Service": "logs.region.amazonaws.com" },
5     "Action": "sts:AssumeRole"
6   }
7 }
```

9. Use the **create-role** command to create the IAM role, specifying the trust policy file. Note of the returned **Role.Arn** value, as you will need it in a later step:

```
1 aws iam create-role \
2       --role-name CWLtoKinesisFirehoseRole \
3       --assume-role-policy-document file://~/TrustPolicyForCWL.json
4
5 {
6     "Role": {
7         "AssumeRolePolicyDocument": {
8             "Statement": {
9                 "Action": "sts:AssumeRole",
10                "Effect": "Allow",
11                "Principal": {
12                    "Service": "logs.region.amazonaws.com"
13                }
14            }
15        },
16        "RoleId": "AAOIIAH450GAB4HC5F431",
17        "CreateDate": "2015-05-29T13:46:29.431Z",
18        "RoleName": "CWLtoKinesisFirehoseRole",
19        "Path": "/",
20        "Arn": "arn:aws:iam::123456789012:role/CWLtoKinesisFirehoseRole"
21    }
22 }
```

10. Create a permissions policy to define what actions CloudWatch Logs can do on your account. First, use a text editor to create a permissions policy file (for example, ~/PermissionsForCWL.json):

```
1  {
2      "Statement":[
3          {
4              "Effect":"Allow",
5              "Action":["firehose:*"],
6              "Resource":["arn:aws:firehose:region:123456789012:*"]
7          },
8          {
9              "Effect":"Allow",
10             "Action":["iam:PassRole"],
11             "Resource":["arn:aws:iam::123456789012:role/CWLtoKinesisFirehoseRole"]
12         }
13     ]
14 }
```

11. Associate the permissions policy with the role using the put-role-policy command:

```
1  aws iam put-role-policy --role-name CWLtoKinesisFirehoseRole --policy-name Permissions-
       Policy-For-CWL --policy-document file://~/PermissionsForCWL.json
```

12. After the Amazon Kinesis Data Firehose delivery stream is in active state and you have created the IAM role, you can create the CloudWatch Logs subscription filter. The subscription filter immediately starts the flow of real-time log data from the chosen log group to your Amazon Kinesis Data Firehose delivery stream:

```
1  aws logs put-subscription-filter \
2      --log-group-name "CloudTrail" \
3      --filter-name "Destination" \
4      --filter-pattern "{$.userIdentity.type = Root}" \
5      --destination-arn "arn:aws:firehose:region:123456789012:deliverystream/my-delivery-
           stream" \
6      --role-arn "arn:aws:iam::123456789012:role/CWLtoKinesisFirehoseRole"
```

13. After you set up the subscription filter, CloudWatch Logs will forward all the incoming log events that match the filter pattern to your Amazon Kinesis Data Firehose delivery stream. Your data will start appearing in your Amazon S3 based on the time buffer interval set on your Amazon Kinesis Data Firehose delivery stream. Once enough time has passed, you can verify your data by checking your Amazon S3 Bucket.

```
1  aws s3api list-objects --bucket 'my-bucket' --prefix 'firehose/'
2
3  {
4      "Contents": [
5          {
6              "LastModified": "2015-10-29T00:01:25.000Z",
7              "ETag": "\"a14589f8897f4089d3264d9e2d1f1610\"",
8              "StorageClass": "STANDARD",
9              "Key": "firehose/2015/10/29/00/my-delivery-stream-2015-10-29-00-01-21-a188030a
                  -62d2-49e6-b7c2-b11f1a7ba250",
10             "Owner": {
11                 "DisplayName": "cloudwatch-logs",
12                 "ID": "1ec9cf700ef6be062b19584e0b7d84ecc19237f87b5"
13             },
14             "Size": 593
15         },
16         {
```

```
17        "LastModified": "2015-10-29T00:35:41.000Z",
18        "ETag": "\"a7035b65872bb2161388ffb63dd1aec5\"",
19        "StorageClass": "STANDARD",
20        "Key": "firehose/2015/10/29/00/my-delivery-stream-2015-10-29-00-35-40-7cc92023
             -7e66-49bc-9fd4-fc9819cc8ed3",
21        "Owner": {
22            "DisplayName": "cloudwatch-logs",
23            "ID": "1ec9cf700ef6be062b19584e0b7d84ecc19237f87b6"
24        },
25        "Size": 5752
26      }
27    ]
28  }
```

```
1 aws s3api get-object --bucket 'my-bucket' --key 'firehose/2015/10/29/00/my-delivery-stream
     -2015-10-29-00-01-21-a188030a-62d2-49e6-b7c2-b11f1a7ba250' testfile.gz
2
3 {
4     "AcceptRanges": "bytes",
5     "ContentType": "application/octet-stream",
6     "LastModified": "Thu, 29 Oct 2015 00:07:06 GMT",
7     "ContentLength": 593,
8     "Metadata": {}
9   }
```

The data in the Amazon S3 object is compressed with the gzip format. You can examine the raw data from the command line using the following Unix command:

```
1 zcat testfile.gz
```

Cross-Account Log Data Sharing with Subscriptions

You can collaborate with an owner of a different AWS account and receive their log events on your AWS resources, such as an Amazon Kinesis stream (this is known as cross-account data sharing). For example, this log event data can be read from a centralized Amazon Kinesis stream to perform custom processing and analysis. Custom processing is especially useful when you collaborate and analyze data across many accounts. For example, a company's information security group might want to analyze data for real-time intrusion detection or anomalous behaviors so it could conduct an audit of accounts in all divisions in the company by collecting their federated production logs for central processing. A real-time stream of event data across those accounts can be assembled and delivered to the information security groups who can use Kinesis to attach the data to their existing security analytic systems.

Kinesis streams are currently the only resource supported as a destination for cross-account subscriptions.

To share log data across accounts, you need to establish a log data sender and receiver:

- **Log data sender**—gets the destination information from the recipient and lets CloudWatch Logs know that it is ready to send its log events to the specified destination. In the procedures in the rest of this section, the log data sender is shown with a fictional AWS account number of 111111111111.
- **Log data recipient**—sets up a destination that encapsulates an Kinesis stream and lets CloudWatch Logs know that the recipient wants to receive log data. The recipient then shares the information about his destination with the sender. In the procedures in the rest of this section, the log data recipient is shown with a fictional AWS account number of 999999999999.

To start receiving log events from cross-account users, the log data recipient first creates a CloudWatch Logs destination. Each destination consists of the following key elements:

Destination name
The name of the destination you want to create.

Target ARN
The Amazon Resource Name (ARN) of the AWS resource that you want to use as the destination of the subscription feed.

Role ARN
An AWS Identity and Access Management (IAM) role that grants CloudWatch Logs the necessary permissions to put data into the chosen Kinesis stream.

Access policy
An IAM policy document (in JSON format, written using IAM policy grammar) that governs the set of users that are allowed to write to your destination.

The log group and the destination must be in the same AWS region. However, the AWS resource that the destination points to can be located in a different region.

Topics

- Create a Destination
- Create a Subscription Filter
- Validating the Flow of Log Events
- Modifying Destination Membership at Runtime

Create a Destination

The steps in this procedure are to be done in the log data recipient account. For this example, the log data recipient account has an AWS account ID of 999999999999, while the log data sender AWS account ID is 111111111111.

This example creates a destination using an Kinesis stream called RecipientStream, and a role that enables CloudWatch Logs to write data to it.

To create a destination

1. Create a destination stream in Kinesis. At a command prompt, type:

```
1  aws kinesis create-stream --stream-name "RecipientStream" --shard-count 1
```

2. Wait until the Kinesis stream becomes active. You can use the **aws kinesis describe-stream** command to check the **StreamDescription.StreamStatus** property. In addition, take note of the **StreamDescription.StreamARN** value because it will be passed to CloudWatch Logs later:

```
1  aws kinesis describe-stream --stream-name "RecipientStream"
2  {
3    "StreamDescription": {
4      "StreamStatus": "ACTIVE",
5      "StreamName": "RecipientStream",
6      "StreamARN": "arn:aws:kinesis:us-east-1:999999999999:stream/RecipientStream",
7      "Shards": [
8        {
9          "ShardId": "shardId-000000000000",
10         "HashKeyRange": {
11           "EndingHashKey": "340282366920938463463374607431768EXAMPLE",
12           "StartingHashKey": "0"
13         },
14         "SequenceNumberRange": {
15           "StartingSequenceNumber": "49551135218688818456679503831981458784591352702189
                 EXAMPLE"
16         }
17       }
18     ]
19   }
20 }
```

It might take a minute or two for your stream to show up in the active state.

3. Create the IAM role that will grant CloudWatch Logs the permission to put data into your Kinesis stream. First, you'll need to create a trust policy in a file ~/**TrustPolicyForCWL.json**. Use a text editor to create this policy file, do not use the IAM console.

```
1  {
2    "Statement": {
3      "Effect": "Allow",
4      "Principal": { "Service": "logs.region.amazonaws.com" },
5      "Action": "sts:AssumeRole"
6    }
7  }
```

4. Use the **aws iam create-role** command to create the IAM role, specifying the trust policy file. Take note of the returned Role.Arn value because that will also be passed to CloudWatch Logs later:

```
1 aws iam create-role \
2     --role-name CWLtoKinesisRole \
3     --assume-role-policy-document file://~/TrustPolicyForCWL.json
4
5 {
6     "Role": {
7         "AssumeRolePolicyDocument": {
8             "Statement": {
9                 "Action": "sts:AssumeRole",
10                "Effect": "Allow",
11                "Principal": {
12                    "Service": "logs.region.amazonaws.com"
13                }
14            }
15        },
16        "RoleId": "AAOIIAH450GAB4HC5F431",
17        "CreateDate": "2015-05-29T13:46:29.431Z",
18        "RoleName": "CWLtoKinesisRole",
19        "Path": "/",
20        "Arn": "arn:aws:iam::999999999999:role/CWLtoKinesisRole"
21    }
22 }
```

5. Create a permissions policy to define which actions CloudWatch Logs can perform on your account. First, you'll use a text editor to create a permissions policy in a file ~/**PermissionsForCWL.json**:

```
1 {
2   "Statement": [
3     {
4       "Effect": "Allow",
5       "Action": "kinesis:PutRecord",
6       "Resource": "arn:aws:kinesis:region:999999999999:stream/RecipientStream"
7     },
8     {
9       "Effect": "Allow",
10      "Action": "iam:PassRole",
11      "Resource": "arn:aws:iam::999999999999:role/CWLtoKinesisRole"
12    }
13  ]
14 }
```

6. Associate the permissions policy with the role using the **aws iam put-role-policy** command:

```
1 aws iam put-role-policy --role-name CWLtoKinesisRole --policy-name Permissions-Policy-For-
    CWL --policy-document file://~/PermissionsForCWL.json
```

7. After the Kinesis stream is in the active state and you have created the IAM role, you can create the CloudWatch Logs destination.

   1. This step will not associate an access policy with your destination and is only the first step out of two that completes a destination creation. Make a note of the **DestinationArn** that is returned in the payload:

```
1 aws logs put-destination \
2     --destination-name "testDestination" \
3     --target-arn "arn:aws:kinesis:region:999999999999:stream/RecipientStream" \
4     --role-arn "arn:aws:iam::999999999999:role/CWLtoKinesisRole"
```

```
 5
 6  {
 7      "DestinationName" : "testDestination",
 8      "RoleArn" : "arn:aws:iam::999999999999:role/CWLtoKinesisRole",
 9      "DestinationArn" : "arn:aws:logs:us-east-1:999999999999:destination:testDestination",
10      "TargetArn" : "arn:aws:kinesis:us-east-1:999999999999:stream/RecipientStream"
11  }
```

2. After step 7a is complete, in the log data recipient account, associate an access policy with the destination. This policy enables the log data sender account (111111111111) to access the destination in the log data recipient account (999999999999). You can use a text editor to put this policy in the ~/**AccessPolicy.json** file:

```
 1  {
 2      "Version" : "2012-10-17",
 3      "Statement" : [
 4          {
 5              "Sid" : "",
 6              "Effect" : "Allow",
 7              "Principal" : {
 8                  "AWS" : "111111111111"
 9              },
10              "Action" : "logs:PutSubscriptionFilter",
11              "Resource" : "arn:aws:logs:region:999999999999:destination:testDestination"
12          }
13      ]
14  }
```

3. This creates a policy that defines who has write access to the destination. This policy must specify the **logs:PutSubscriptionFilter** action to access the destination. Cross-account users will use the **PutSubscriptionFilter** action to send log events to the destination:

```
 1  aws logs put-destination-policy \
 2      --destination-name "testDestination" \
 3      --access-policy file://~/AccessPolicy.json
```

This access policy allows the root user of the AWS Account with ID 111111111111 to call **PutSubscriptionFilter** against the destination with ARN arn:aws:logs:*region*:999999999999:destination:testDestination. Any other user's attempt to call PutSubscriptionFilter against this destination will be rejected.

To validate a user's privileges against an access policy, see Using Policy Validator in the *IAM User Guide*.

Create a Subscription Filter

After you create a destination, the log data recipient account can share the destination ARN (arn:aws:logs:us-east-1:999999999999:destination:testDestination) with other AWS accounts so that they can send log events to the same destination. These other sending accounts users then create a subscription filter on their respective log groups against this destination. The subscription filter immediately starts the flow of real-time log data from the chosen log group to the specified destination.

In the following example, a subscription filter is associated with a log group containing AWS CloudTrail events so that every logged activity made by "Root" AWS credentials is delivered to the destination you created above that encapsulates an Kinesis stream called "RecipientStream". For more information about how to send AWS CloudTrail events to CloudWatch Logs, see Sending CloudTrail Events to CloudWatch Logs in the *AWS CloudTrail User Guide*.

```
1 aws logs put-subscription-filter \
2     --log-group-name "CloudTrail" \
3     --filter-name "RecipientStream" \
4     --filter-pattern "{$.userIdentity.type = Root}" \
5     --destination-arn "arn:aws:logs:region:999999999999:destination:testDestination"
```

The log group and the destination must be in the same AWS region. However, the destination can point to an AWS resource such as a Kinesis stream that is located in a different region.

Note

Unlike the subscriptions example Real-time Processing of Log Data with Subscriptions, in this example you did not have to provide a role-arn. This is because role-arn is needed for impersonation while writing to an Kinesis stream, which has already been provided by the destination owner while creating destination.

Validating the Flow of Log Events

After you create the subscription filter, CloudWatch Logs forwards all the incoming log events that match the filter pattern to the Kinesis stream that is encapsulated within the destination stream called "**RecipientStream**". The destination owner can verify that this is happening by using the **aws kinesis get-shard-iterator** command to grab an Kinesis shard, and using the **aws kinesis get-records** command to fetch some Kinesis records:

```
1  aws kinesis get-shard-iterator \
2      --stream-name RecipientStream \
3      --shard-id shardId-000000000000 \
4      --shard-iterator-type TRIM_HORIZON
5
6  {
7      "ShardIterator":
8      "AAAAAAAAAAFGU/
           kLvNggvndHq2UIFOw5PZc6F01s3e3afsSscRM70JSbjIefg2ub07nk1y6CDxYR1UoGHJNP4m4NFUetzfL+wev+
           e2P4djJg4L9wmXKvQYoE+rMUiFq+p4Cn3IgvqOb5dRAOyybNdRcdzvnC35KQANoHzzahKdRGb9v4scv+3vaq+f+
           OIK8zM5My8ID+g6rMo7UKWeI4+IWiKEXAMPLE"
9  }
10
11 aws kinesis get-records \
12     --limit 10 \
13     --shard-iterator
14     "AAAAAAAAAAFGU/
           kLvNggvndHq2UIFOw5PZc6F01s3e3afsSscRM70JSbjIefg2ub07nk1y6CDxYR1UoGHJNP4m4NFUetzfL+wev+
           e2P4djJg4L9wmXKvQYoE+rMUiFq+p4Cn3IgvqOb5dRAOyybNdRcdzvnC35KQANoHzzahKdRGb9v4scv+3vaq+f
           +OIK8zM5My8ID+g6rMo7UKWeI4+IWiKEXAMPLE"
```

Note

You may need to rerun the get-records command a few times before Kinesis starts to return data.

You should see a response with an array of Kinesis records. The data attribute in the Kinesis record is Base64 encoded and compressed in gzip format. You can examine the raw data from the command line using the following Unix command:

```
1  echo -n "<Content of Data>" | base64 -d | zcat
```

The Base64 decoded and decompressed data is formatted as JSON with the following structure:

```
1  {
2      "owner": "111111111111",
3      "logGroup": "CloudTrail",
4      "logStream": "111111111111_CloudTrail_us-east-1",
5      "subscriptionFilters": [
6          "RecipientStream"
7      ],
8      "messageType": "DATA_MESSAGE",
9      "logEvents": [
10         {
11             "id": "31953106606969698337880902507980421114328961542429EXAMPLE",
12             "timestamp": 1432826855000,
13             "message": "{\"eventVersion\":\"1.03\",\"userIdentity\":{\"type\":\"Root\"}"
14         },
15         {
16             "id": "31953106606969698337880902507980421114328961542429EXAMPLE",
17             "timestamp": 1432826855000,
```

```
18          "message": "{\"eventVersion\":\"1.03\",\"userIdentity\":{\"type\":\"Root\"}"
19      },
20      {
21          "id": "31953106060696698337880902507980421114328961542429EXAMPLE",
22          "timestamp": 1432826855000,
23          "message": "{\"eventVersion\":\"1.03\",\"userIdentity\":{\"type\":\"Root\"}"
24      }
25      ]
26  }
```

The key elements in this data structure are as follows:

owner
The AWS Account ID of the originating log data.

logGroup
The log group name of the originating log data.

logStream
The log stream name of the originating log data.

subscriptionFilters
The list of subscription filter names that matched with the originating log data.

messageType
Data messages will use the "DATA_MESSAGE" type. Sometimes CloudWatch Logs may emit Kinesis records with a "CONTROL_MESSAGE" type, mainly for checking if the destination is reachable.

logEvents
The actual log data, represented as an array of log event records. The ID property is a unique identifier for every log event.

Modifying Destination Membership at Runtime

You might encounter situations where you have to add or remove membership of some users from a destination that you own. You can use the **PutDestinationPolicy** action on your destination with new access policy. In the following example, a previously added account **111111111111** is stopped from sending any more log data, and account **222222222222** is enabled.

1. Fetch the policy that is currently associated with the destination **testDestination** and make a note of the **AccessPolicy**:

```
1  aws logs describe-destinations \
2      --destination-name-prefix "testDestination"
3
4  {
5    "Destinations": [
6      {
7        "DestinationName": "testDestination",
8        "RoleArn": "arn:aws:iam::123456789012:role/CWLtoKinesisRole",
9        "DestinationArn": "arn:aws:logs:region:999999999999:destination:testDestination",
10       "TargetArn": "arn:aws:kinesis:region:999999999999:stream/RecipientStream",
11       "AccessPolicy": "{\"Version\": \"2012-10-17\", \"Statement\": [{\"Sid\": \"\", \"
           Effect\": \"Allow\", \"Principal\": {\"AWS\": \"234567890123\"}, \"Action\": \"
           logs:PutSubscriptionFilter\", \"Resource\": \"arn:aws:logs:region:123456789012:
           destination:testDestination\"}] }"
12     }
13   ]
14 }
```

2. Update the policy to reflect that account **111111111111** is stopped, and that account **222222222222** is enabled. Put this policy in the ~/**NewAccessPolicy.json** file:

```
1  {
2    "Version" : "2012-10-17",
3    "Statement" : [
4      {
5        "Sid" : "",
6        "Effect" : "Allow",
7        "Principal" : {
8          "AWS" : "222222222222"
9        },
10       "Action" : "logs:PutSubscriptionFilter",
11       "Resource" : "arn:aws:logs:region:123456789012:destination:testDestination"
12     }
13   ]
14 }
```

3. Call **PutDestinationPolicy** to associate the policy defined in the **NewAccessPolicy.json** file with the destination:

```
1  aws logs put-destination-policy \
2  --destination-name "testDestination" \
3  --access-policy file://~/NewAccessPolicy.json
```

This will eventually disable the log events from account ID **111111111111**. Log events from account ID **222222222222** start flowing to the destination as soon as the owner of account **222222222222** creates a subscription filter using **PutSubscriptionFilter**.

Exporting Log Data to Amazon S3

You can export log data from your log groups to an Amazon S3 bucket and use this data in custom processing and analysis, or to load onto other systems.

To begin the export process, you must create an S3 bucket to store the exported log data. You can store the exported files in your Amazon S3 bucket and define Amazon S3 lifecycle rules to archive or delete exported files automatically.

You can export logs from multiple log groups or multiple time ranges to the same S3 bucket. To separate log data for each export task, you can specify a prefix that will be used as the Amazon S3 key prefix for all exported objects.

Log data can take up to 12 hours to become available for export. For near real-time analysis of log data, see Real-time Processing of Log Data with Subscriptions instead.

Topics

- Concepts
- Export Log Data to Amazon S3 Using the Console
- Export Log Data to Amazon S3 Using the AWS CLI

Concepts

Before you begin, become familiar with the following export concepts:

log group name
The name of the log group associated with an export task. The log data in this log group will be exported to the specified Amazon S3 bucket.

from (timestamp)
A required timestamp expressed as the number of milliseconds since Jan 1, 1970 00:00:00 UTC. All log events in the log group that were ingested after this time will be exported.

to (timestamp)
A required timestamp expressed as the number of milliseconds since Jan 1, 1970 00:00:00 UTC. All log events in the log group that were ingested before this time will be exported.

destination bucket
The name of the Amazon S3 bucket associated with an export task. This bucket is used to export the log data from the specified log group.

destination prefix
An optional attribute that is used as the S3 key prefix for all exported objects. This helps create a folder-like organization in your bucket.

Export Log Data to Amazon S3 Using the Console

In the following example, you'll use the Amazon CloudWatch console to export all data from an Amazon CloudWatch Logs log group named "my-log-group" to an Amazon S3 bucket named "my-exported-logs."

Step 1: Create an Amazon S3 Bucket

We recommend that you use a bucket that was created specifically for CloudWatch Logs. However, if you want to use an existing bucket, you can skip to step 2.

Note
The Amazon S3 bucket must reside in the same region as the log data to export. CloudWatch Logs does not support exporting data to Amazon S3 buckets in a different region.

To create an Amazon S3 bucket

1. Open the Amazon S3 console at https://console.aws.amazon.com/s3/.

2. If necessary, change the region. From the navigation bar, choose the region where your CloudWatch Logs reside.

3. Choose **Create Bucket**.

4. For **Bucket Name**, type a name for the bucket.

5. For **Region**, select the region where your CloudWatch Logs data resides.

6. Choose **Create**.

Step 2: Set Permissions on an Amazon S3 Bucket

By default, all Amazon S3 buckets and objects are private. Only the resource owner, the AWS account that created the bucket, can access the bucket and any objects it contains. However, the resource owner can choose to grant access permissions to other resources and users by writing an access policy.

When you set the policy, we recommend you include a randomly-generated string as the prefix for the bucket, so that only intended log streams are exported to the bucket.

To set permissions on an Amazon S3 bucket

1. In the Amazon S3 console, choose the bucket that you created in Step 1.

2. Choose **Permissions, Bucket policy**.

3. In the **Bucket Policy Editor** dialog box, add the following policy, changing `my-exported-logs` to the name of your S3 bucket and `random-string` to a randomly-generated string of characters. Be sure to specify the correct region endpoint for **Principal**.

```
1  {
2      "Version": "2012-10-17",
3      "Statement": [
4        {
5            "Action": "s3:GetBucketAcl",
6            "Effect": "Allow",
7            "Resource": "arn:aws:s3:::my-exported-logs",
8            "Principal": { "Service": "logs.us-west-2.amazonaws.com" }
9        },
10       {
11           "Action": "s3:PutObject" ,
```

```
12          "Effect": "Allow",
13          "Resource": "arn:aws:s3:::my-exported-logs/random-string/*",
14          "Condition": { "StringEquals": { "s3:x-amz-acl": "bucket-owner-full-control" } },
15          "Principal": { "Service": "logs.us-west-2.amazonaws.com" }
16      }
17    ]
18 }
```

4. Choose **Save** to set the policy that you just added as the access policy on your bucket. This policy enables CloudWatch Logs to export log data to your Amazon S3 bucket. The bucket owner has full permissions on all of the exported objects. **Warning**
   If the existing bucket already has one or more policies attached to it, add the statements for CloudWatch Logs access to that policy or policies. We recommend that you evaluate the resulting set of permissions to be sure that they are appropriate for the users who will access the bucket.

Step 3: Create an Export Task

In this step you create the export task for exporting logs from a log group.

To export data to Amazon S3 using the CloudWatch console

1. Open the CloudWatch console at https://console.aws.amazon.com/cloudwatch/.

2. In the navigation pane, choose **Logs**.

3. On the **Log Groups** screen, select the button next to a log group, and then choose **Actions, Export data to Amazon S3**.

4. On the **Export data to Amazon S3** screen, under **Define data to export**, set the time range for the data to export using **From** and **To**.

5. If your log group has multiple log streams, you can provide a log stream prefix to limit the log group data to a specific stream. Choose **Advanced**, and then for **Stream prefix**, type the log stream prefix.

6. Under **Choose S3 bucket**, choose the account associated with the Amazon S3 bucket.

7. For **S3 bucket name**, choose an Amazon S3 bucket.

8. Choose **Advanced**, and then for **S3 Bucket prefix**, type the randomly-generated string you specified in the bucket policy.

9. Choose **Export data** to export your log data to Amazon S3.

10. To view the status of the log data that you exported to Amazon S3, choose **Actions, View all exports to Amazon S3**.

Export Log Data to Amazon S3 Using the AWS CLI

In the following example, you'll use an export task to export all data from a CloudWatch Logs log group named "my-log-group" to an Amazon S3 bucket named "my-exported-logs." This example assumes that you have already created a log group called "my-log-group".

Step 1: Create an Amazon S3 Bucket

We recommend that you use a bucket that was created specifically for CloudWatch Logs. However, if you want to use an existing bucket, you can skip to step 2.

Note
The Amazon S3 bucket must reside in the same region as the log data to export. CloudWatch Logs does not support exporting data to Amazon S3 buckets in a different region.

To create an Amazon S3 bucket using the AWS CLI
At a command prompt, run the following create-bucket command, where `LocationConstraint` is the region where you are exporting log data:

```
1 aws s3api create-bucket --bucket my-exported-logs --create-bucket-configuration
     LocationConstraint=us-east-2
```

The following is example output:

```
1 {
2     "Location": "/my-exported-logs"
3 }
```

Step 2: Set Permissions on an Amazon S3 Bucket

By default, all Amazon S3 buckets and objects are private. Only the resource owner, the AWS account that created the bucket, can access the bucket and any objects it contains. However, the resource owner can choose to grant access permissions to other resources and users by writing an access policy.

To set permissions on an Amazon S3 bucket

1. Create a file named policy.json and add the following access policy, changing `Resource` to the name of your S3 bucket and `Principal` to the endpoint of the region where you are exporting log data. Use a text editor to create this policy file. Do not use the IAM console.

```
1  {
2      "Version": "2012-10-17",
3      "Statement": [
4          {
5              "Action": "s3:GetBucketAcl",
6              "Effect": "Allow",
7              "Resource": "arn:aws:s3:::my-exported-logs",
8              "Principal": { "Service": "logs.us-west-2.amazonaws.com" }
9          },
10         {
11             "Action": "s3:PutObject" ,
12             "Effect": "Allow",
13             "Resource": "arn:aws:s3:::my-exported-logs/*",
14             "Condition": { "StringEquals": { "s3:x-amz-acl": "bucket-owner-full-control" }
                   },
```

```
15              "Principal": { "Service": "logs.us-west-2.amazonaws.com" }
16          }
17      ]
18  }
```

2. Set the policy that you just added as the access policy on your bucket using the put-bucket-policy command. This policy enables CloudWatch Logs to export log data to your Amazon S3 bucket. The bucket owner will have full permissions on all of the exported objects.

```
1 aws s3api put-bucket-policy --bucket my-exported-logs --policy file://policy.json
```

Warning
If the existing bucket already has one or more policies attached to it, add the statements for CloudWatch Logs access to that policy or policies. We recommend that you evaluate the resulting set of permissions to be sure that they are appropriate for the users who will access the bucket.

Step 3: Create an Export Task

After you create the export task for exporting logs from a log group, the export task might take anywhere from a few seconds to a few hours, depending on the size of the data to export.

To create an export task using the AWS CLI
At a command prompt, use the following create-export-task command to create the export task:

```
1 aws logs create-export-task --task-name "my-log-group-09-10-2015" --log-group-name "my-log-group
  " --from 1441490400000 --to 1441494000000 --destination "my-exported-logs" --destination-
  prefix "export-task-output"
```

The following is example output:

```
1 {
2     "task-id": "cda45419-90ea-4db5-9833-aade86253e66"
3 }
```

Step 4: Describe Export Tasks

After you create an export task, you can get the current status of the task.

To describe export tasks using the AWS CLI
At a command prompt, use the following describe-export-tasks command:

```
1 aws logs describe-export-tasks --task-id "cda45419-90ea-4db5-9833-aade86253e66"
```

The following is example output:

```
1 {
2     "ExportTasks": [
3     {
4         "Destination": "my-exported-logs",
5         "DestinationPrefix": "export-task-output",
6         "ExecutionInfo": {
7             "CreationTime": 1441495400000
8         },
9         "From": 1441490400000,
10        "LogGroupName": "my-log-group",
11        "Status": {
```

```
12       "Code": "RUNNING",
13       "Message": "Started Successfully"
14     },
15     "TaskId": "cda45419-90ea-4db5-9833-aade86253e66",
16     "TaskName": "my-log-group-09-10-2015",
17     "To": 1441494000000
18   }]
19 }
```

You can use the `describe-export-tasks` command in three different ways:

- Without any filters: Lists all of your export tasks, in reverse order of creation.
- Filter on task ID: Lists the export task, if one exists, with the specified ID.
- Filter on task status: Lists the export tasks with the specified status.

For example, use the following command to filter on the FAILED status:

```
1 aws logs describe-export-tasks --status-code "FAILED"
```

The following is example output:

```
1 {
2   "ExportTasks": [
3     {
4       "Destination": "my-exported-logs",
5       "DestinationPrefix": "export-task-output",
6       "ExecutionInfo": {
7         "CompletionTime": 1441498600000
8         "CreationTime": 1441495400000
9       },
10      "From": 1441490400000,
11      "LogGroupName": "my-log-group",
12      "Status": {
13        "Code": "FAILED",
14        "Message": "FAILED"
15      },
16      "TaskId": "cda45419-90ea-4db5-9833-aade86253e66",
17      "TaskName": "my-log-group-09-10-2015",
18      "To": 1441494000000
19    }]
20 }
```

Step 5: Cancel an Export Task

You can cancel an export task if it is in either the PENDING or the RUNNING state.

To cancel an export task using the AWS CLI
At a command prompt, use the following cancel-export-task command:

```
1 aws logs cancel-export-task --task-id "cda45419-90ea-4db5-9833-aade86253e66"
```

Note that you can use the describe-export-tasks command to verify that the task was canceled successfully.

Streaming CloudWatch Logs Data to Amazon Elasticsearch Service

You can configure a CloudWatch Logs log group to stream data it receives to your Amazon Elasticsearch Service (Amazon ES) cluster in near real-time through a CloudWatch Logs subscription. For more information, see Real-time Processing of Log Data with Subscriptions.

Note
Streaming large amounts of CloudWatch Logs data to Amazon ES might result in high usage charges. We recommend that you monitor your AWS bill to help avoid higher-than-expected charges. For more information, see Monitor Your Estimated Charges Using CloudWatch.

Prerequisites

Before you begin, create an Amazon ES domain. The Amazon ES domain can have either public access or VPC access, but you cannot then modify the type of access after the domain is created. You might want to review your Amazon ES domain settings later, and modify your cluster configuration based on the amount of data your cluster will be processing.

For more information about Amazon ES, see the Amazon Elasticsearch Service Developer Guide.

To create an Amazon ES domain
At a command prompt, use the following create-elasticsearch-domain command:

```
1 aws es create-elasticsearch-domain --domain-name my-domain
```

Subscribe a Log Group to Amazon ES

You can use the CloudWatch console to subscribe a log group to Amazon ES.

To subscribe a log group to Amazon ES

1. Open the CloudWatch console at https://console.aws.amazon.com/cloudwatch/.

2. In the navigation pane, choose **Logs**.

3. Select the log group to subscribe.

4. Choose **Actions, Stream to Amazon Elasticsearch Service**.

5. On the **Start Streaming to Amazon Elasticsearch Service** screen, for **Amazon ES cluster**, choose the cluster you created in the previous step, and then choose **Next**.

6. Under **Lambda Function**, for **Lambda IAM Execution Role**, choose the IAM role that Lambda should use when executing calls to Amazon ES, and then choose **Next**.

   The IAM role you choose must fulfill these requirements:

   - It must have `lambda.amazonaws.com` in the trust relationship.

   - It must include the following policy:

```
1 {
2     "Version": "2012-10-17",
3     "Statement": [
4         {
5             "Action": [
6                 "es:*"
7             ],
8             "Effect": "Allow",
```

93

```
 9              "Resource": "arn:aws:es:region:account-id:domain/target-domain-name/*"
10          }
11      ]
12 }
```

- If the target Amazon ES domain uses VPC access, the role must have the ** AWSLambdaVPCAccessExecutionRole** policy attached. This Amazon-managed policy grants Lambda access to the customer's VPC, enabling Lambda to write to the Amazon ES endpoint in the VPC.

7. On the **Configure Log Format and Filters** screen, for **Log Format**, choose a log format.

8. Under **Subscription Filter Pattern**, type the terms or pattern to find in your log events. This ensures that you send only the data you are interested in to your Amazon ES cluster. For more information, see Searching and Filtering Log Data.

9. (Optional) Under **Select Log Data to Test**, select a log stream and then click **Test Pattern** to verify that your search filter is returning the results you expect.

10. Choose **Next**, and then on the **Review & Start Streaming to Amazon Elasticsearch Service** screen, choose **Start Streaming**.

Authentication and Access Control for Amazon CloudWatch Logs

Access to Amazon CloudWatch Logs requires credentials that AWS can use to authenticate your requests. Those credentials must have permissions to access AWS resources, such as to retrieve CloudWatch Logs data about your cloud resources. The following sections provide details on how you can use AWS Identity and Access Management (IAM) and CloudWatch Logs to help secure your resources by controlling who can access them:

- Authentication
- Access Control

Authentication

You can access AWS as any of the following types of identities:

- **AWS account root user** – When you sign up for AWS, you provide an email address and password that is associated with your AWS account. These are your *root credentials* and they provide complete access to all of your AWS resources. **Important**
  For security reasons, we recommend that you use the root credentials only to create an *administrator user*, which is an *IAM user* with full permissions to your AWS account. Then, you can use this administrator user to create other IAM users and roles with limited permissions. For more information, see IAM Best Practices and Creating an Admin User and Group in the *IAM User Guide*.

- **IAM user** – An IAM user is simply an identity within your AWS account that has specific custom permissions (for example, permissions to view metrics in CloudWatch Logs). You can use an IAM user name and password to sign in to secure AWS webpages like the AWS Management Console, AWS Discussion Forums, or the AWS Support Center.

  In addition to a user name and password, you can also generate access keys for each user. You can use these keys when you access AWS services programmatically, either through one of the several SDKs or by using the AWS Command Line Interface (AWS CLI). The SDK and CLI tools use the access keys to cryptographically sign your request. If you don't use the AWS tools, you must sign the request yourself. CloudWatch Logs supports *Signature Version 4*, a protocol for authenticating inbound API requests. For more information about authenticating requests, see Signature Version 4 Signing Process in the *AWS General Reference*.

- **IAM role** – An IAM role is another IAM identity you can create in your account that has specific permissions. It is similar to an *IAM user*, but it is not associated with a specific person. An IAM role enables you to obtain temporary access keys that can be used to access AWS services and resources. IAM roles with temporary credentials are useful in the following situations:

  - **Federated user access** – Instead of creating an IAM user, you can use preexisting user identities from AWS Directory Service, your enterprise user directory, or a web identity provider. These are known as *federated users*. AWS assigns a role to a federated user when access is requested through an identity provider. For more information about federated users, see Federated Users and Roles in the *IAM User Guide*.

  - **Cross-account access** – You can use an IAM role in your account to grant another AWS account permissions to access your account's resources. For an example, see Tutorial: Delegate Access Across AWS Accounts Using IAM Roles in the *IAM User Guide*.

- **AWS service access** – You can use an IAM role in your account to grant an AWS service permissions to access your account's resources. For example, you can create a role that allows Amazon Redshift to access an Amazon S3 bucket on your behalf and then load data stored in the bucket into an Amazon Redshift cluster. For more information, see Creating a Role to Delegate Permissions to an AWS Service in the *IAM User Guide*.

- **Applications running on Amazon EC2** – Instead of storing access keys within the EC2 instance for use by applications running on the instance and making AWS API requests, you can use an IAM role to manage temporary credentials for these applications. To assign an AWS role to an EC2 instance and make it available to all of its applications, you can create an instance profile that is attached to the instance. An instance profile contains the role and enables programs running on the EC2 instance to get temporary credentials. For more information, see Using Roles for Applications on Amazon EC2 in the *IAM User Guide*.

Access Control

You can have valid credentials to authenticate your requests, but unless you have permissions you cannot create or access CloudWatch Logs resources. For example, you must have permissions to create log streams, create log groups, and so on.

The following sections describe how to manage permissions for CloudWatch Logs. We recommend that you read the overview first.

- Overview of Managing Access Permissions to Your CloudWatch Logs Resources
- Using Identity-Based Policies (IAM Policies) for CloudWatch Logs
- CloudWatch Logs Permissions Reference

Overview of Managing Access Permissions to Your CloudWatch Logs Resources

Every AWS resource is owned by an AWS account, and permissions to create or access a resource are governed by permissions policies. An account administrator can attach permissions policies to IAM identities (that is, users, groups, and roles), and some services (such as AWS Lambda) also support attaching permissions policies to resources.

Note

An *account administrator* (or administrator IAM user) is a user with administrator privileges. For more information, see IAM Best Practices in the *IAM User Guide*.

When granting permissions, you decide who is getting the permissions, the resources they get permissions for, and the specific actions that you want to allow on those resources.

Topics

- CloudWatch Logs Resources and Operations
- Understanding Resource Ownership
- Managing Access to Resources
- Specifying Policy Elements: Actions, Effects, and Principals
- Specifying Conditions in a Policy

CloudWatch Logs Resources and Operations

In CloudWatch Logs the primary resources are log groups, log streams and destinations. CloudWatch Logs does not support subresources (other resources for use with the primary resource).

These resources and subresources have unique Amazon Resource Names (ARNs) associated with them as shown in the following table.

Resource Type	ARN Format
Log group	arn:aws:logs:*region*:*account-id*:log-group:*log_group_name*
Log stream	arn:aws:logs:*region*:*account-id*:log-group:*log_group_name*:log-stream:*log-stream-name*
Destination	arn:aws:logs:*region*:*account-id*:destination:*destination_name*

For more information about ARNs, see ARNs in *IAM User Guide*. For information about CloudWatch Logs ARNs, see Amazon Resource Names (ARNs) and AWS Service Namespaces in *Amazon Web Services General Reference*. For an example of a policy that covers CloudWatch Logs, see Using Identity-Based Policies (IAM Policies) for CloudWatch Logs.

CloudWatch Logs provides a set of operations to work with the CloudWatch Logs resources. For a list of available operations, see CloudWatch Logs Permissions Reference.

Understanding Resource Ownership

The AWS account owns the resources that are created in the account, regardless of who created the resources. Specifically, the resource owner is the AWS account of the principal entity (that is, the root account, an IAM user, or an IAM role) that authenticates the resource creation request. The following examples illustrate how this works:

- If you use the root account credentials of your AWS account to create a log group, your AWS account is the owner of the CloudWatch Logs resource.
- If you create an IAM user in your AWS account and grant permissions to create CloudWatch Logs resources to that user, the user can create CloudWatch Logs resources. However, your AWS account, to which the user belongs, owns the CloudWatch Logs resources.
- If you create an IAM role in your AWS account with permissions to create CloudWatch Logs resources, anyone who can assume the role can create CloudWatch Logs resources. Your AWS account, to which the role belongs, owns the CloudWatch Logs resources.

Managing Access to Resources

A *permissions policy* describes who has access to what. The following section explains the available options for creating permissions policies.

Note
This section discusses using IAM in the context of CloudWatch Logs. It doesn't provide detailed information about the IAM service. For complete IAM documentation, see What Is IAM? in the *IAM User Guide*. For information about IAM policy syntax and descriptions, see IAM Policy Reference in the *IAM User Guide*.

Policies attached to an IAM identity are referred to as identity-based policies (IAM polices) and policies attached to a resource are referred to as resource-based policies. CloudWatch Logs supports identity-based policies, and resource-based policies for destinations, which are used to enable cross account subscriptions. For more information, see Cross-Account Log Data Sharing with Subscriptions.

Topics

- Identity-Based Policies (IAM Policies)
- Resource-Based Policies

Identity-Based Policies (IAM Policies)

You can attach policies to IAM identities. For example, you can do the following:

- **Attach a permissions policy to a user or a group in your account** – To grant a user permissions to view logs in the CloudWatch Logs, console you can attach a permissions policy to a user or group that the user belongs to.

- **Attach a permissions policy to a role (grant cross-account permissions)** – You can attach an identity-based permissions policy to an IAM role to grant cross-account permissions. For example, the administrator in Account A can create a role to grant cross-account permissions to another AWS account (for example, Account B) or an AWS service as follows:

  1. Account A administrator creates an IAM role and attaches a permissions policy to the role that grants permissions on resources in Account A.

  2. Account A administrator attaches a trust policy to the role identifying Account B as the principal who can assume the role.

  3. Account B administrator can then delegate permissions to assume the role to any users in Account B. Doing this allows users in Account B to create or access resources in Account A. The principal in the trust policy an also be an AWS service principal if you want to grant an AWS service permissions to assume the role.

  For more information about using IAM to delegate permissions, see Access Management in the *IAM User Guide*.

The following is an example policy that grants permissions for the `logs:PutLogEvents`, `logs:CreateLogGroup`, and `logs:CreateLogStream` actions on all resources in us-east-1. For log groups, CloudWatch Logs supports identifying specific resources using the resource ARNs (also referred to as resource-level permissions) for some of the API actions. If you want to include all log groups, you must specify the wildcard character (*).

```
1  {
2      "Version":"2012-10-17",
3      "Statement":[
4          {
5              "Sid":"",
6              "Effect":"Allow",
7              "Principal":{
8                  "AWS":"234567890123"
9              },
10             "Action":[
11                 "logs:PutLogEvents",
12                 "logs:CreateLogGroup",
13                 "logs:CreateLogStream"
14             ],
15             "Resource":"arn:aws:logs:us-east-1:*:*"
16         }
17     ]
18 }
```

For more information about using identity-based policies with CloudWatch Logs, see Using Identity-Based Policies (IAM Policies) for CloudWatch Logs. For more information about users, groups, roles, and permissions, see Identities (Users, Groups, and Roles) in the *IAM User Guide*.

Resource-Based Policies

CloudWatch Logs supports resource-based policies for destinations, which you can use to enable cross account subscriptions. For more information, see Create a Destination. Destinations can be created using the PutDestination API, and you can add a resource policy to the destination using the PutDestination API. The following example allows another AWS account with the account ID 111122223333 to subscribe their log groups to the destination `arn:aws:logs:us-east-1:123456789012:destination:testDestination`.

```
1  {
2    "Version" : "2012-10-17",
3    "Statement" : [
4      {
5        "Sid" : "",
6        "Effect" : "Allow",
7        "Principal" : {
8          "AWS" : "111122223333"
9        },
10       "Action" : "logs:PutSubscriptionFilter",
11       "Resource" : "arn:aws:logs:us-east-1:123456789012:destination:testDestination"
12     }
13   ]
14 }
```

Specifying Policy Elements: Actions, Effects, and Principals

For each CloudWatch Logs resource, the service defines a set of API operations. To grant permissions for these API operations, CloudWatch Logs defines a set of actions that you can specify in a policy. Some API operations can require permissions for more than one action in order to perform the API operation. For more information about resources and API operations, see CloudWatch Logs Resources and Operations and CloudWatch Logs Permissions Reference.

The following are the basic policy elements:

- **Resource** – You use an Amazon Resource Name (ARN) to identify the resource that the policy applies to. For more information, see CloudWatch Logs Resources and Operations.
- **Action** – You use action keywords to identify resource operations that you want to allow or deny. For example, the `logs.DescribeLogGroups` permission allows the user permissions to perform the `DescribeLogGroups` operation.
- **Effect** – You specify the effect, either allow or deny, when the user requests the specific action. If you don't explicitly grant access to (allow) a resource, access is implicitly denied. You can also explicitly deny access to a resource, which you might do to make sure that a user cannot access it, even if a different policy grants access.
- **Principal** – In identity-based policies (IAM policies), the user that the policy is attached to is the implicit principal. For resource-based policies, you specify the user, account, service, or other entity that you want to receive permissions (applies to resource-based policies only). CloudWatch Logs supports resource-based policies for destinations.

To learn more about IAM policy syntax and descriptions, see AWS IAM Policy Reference in the *IAM User Guide*.

For a table showing all of the CloudWatch Logs API actions and the resources that they apply to, see CloudWatch Logs Permissions Reference.

Specifying Conditions in a Policy

When you grant permissions, you can use the access policy language to specify the conditions when a policy should take effect. For example, you might want a policy to be applied only after a specific date. For more information about specifying conditions in a policy language, see Condition in the *IAM User Guide*.

To express conditions, you use predefined condition keys. For a list of context keys supported by each AWS service and a list of AWS-wide policy keys, see AWS Service Actions and Condition Context Keys and Global and IAM Condition Context Keys in the *IAM User Guide*.

Using Identity-Based Policies (IAM Policies) for CloudWatch Logs

This topic provides examples of identity-based policies in which an account administrator can attach permissions policies to IAM identities (that is, users, groups, and roles).

Important
We recommend that you first review the introductory topics that explain the basic concepts and options available for you to manage access to your CloudWatch Logs resources. For more information, see Overview of Managing Access Permissions to Your CloudWatch Logs Resources.

This topic covers the following:

- Permissions Required to Use the CloudWatch Console
- AWS Managed (Predefined) Policies for CloudWatch Logs
- Customer Managed Policy Examples

The following is an example of a permissions policy:

```
1  {
2    "Version": "2012-10-17",
3    "Statement": [
4      {
5        "Effect": "Allow",
6        "Action": [
7          "logs:CreateLogGroup",
8          "logs:CreateLogStream",
9          "logs:PutLogEvents",
10         "logs:DescribeLogStreams"
11       ],
12       "Resource": [
13         "arn:aws:logs:*:*:*"
14       ]
15     }
16   ]
17 }
```

This policy has one statement that grants permissions to create log groups and log streams, to upload log events to log streams, and to list details about log streams.

The wildcard character (*) at the end of the `Resource` value means that the statement allows permission for the `logs:CreateLogGroup`, `logs:CreateLogStream`, `logs:PutLogEvents`, and `logs:DescribeLogStreams` actions on any log group. To limit this permission to a specific log group, replace the wildcard character (*) in the resource ARN with the specific log group ARN. For more information about the sections within an IAM policy statement, see IAM Policy Elements Reference in *IAM User Guide*. For a list showing all of the CloudWatch Logs actions, see CloudWatch Logs Permissions Reference.

Permissions Required to Use the CloudWatch Console

For a user to work with CloudWatch Logs in the CloudWatch console, that user must have a minimum set of permissions that allows the user to describe other AWS resources in their AWS account. In order to use CloudWatch Logs in the CloudWatch console, you must have permissions from the following services:

- CloudWatch
- CloudWatch Logs
- Amazon ES
- IAM
- Kinesis

- Lambda
- Amazon S3

If you create an IAM policy that is more restrictive than the minimum required permissions, the console won't function as intended for users with that IAM policy. To ensure that those users can still use the CloudWatch console, also attach the `CloudWatchReadOnlyAccess` managed policy to the user, as described in AWS Managed (Predefined) Policies for CloudWatch Logs.

You don't need to allow minimum console permissions for users that are making calls only to the AWS CLI or the CloudWatch Logs API.

The full set of permissions required to work with the CloudWatch console for a user who is not using the console to manage log subscriptions are:

- cloudwatch:getMetricData
- cloudwatch:listMetrics
- logs:cancelExportTask
- logs:createExportTask
- logs:createLogGroup
- logs:createLogStream
- logs:deleteLogGroup
- logs:deleteLogStream
- logs:deleteMetricFilter
- logs:deleteRetentionPolicy
- logs:deleteSubscriptionFilter
- logs:describeExportTasks
- logs:describeLogGroups
- logs:describeLogStreams
- logs:describeMetricFilters
- logs:describeSubscriptionFilters
- logs:filterLogEvents
- logs:getLogEvents
- logs:putMetricFilter
- logs:putRetentionPolicy
- logs:putSubscriptionFilter
- logs:testMetricFilter

For a user who will also be using the console to manage log subscriptions, the following permissions are also required:

- es:describeElasticsearchDomain
- es:listDomainNames
- iam:attachRolePolicy
- iam:createRole
- iam:getPolicy
- iam:getPolicyVersion
- iam:getRole
- iam:listAttachedRolePolicies
- iam:listRoles
- kinesis:describeStreams
- kinesis:listStreams
- lambda:addPermission
- lambda:createFunction
- lambda:getFunctionConfiguration
- lambda:listAliases
- lambda:listFunctions
- lambda:listVersionsByFunction

- lambda:removePermission
- s3:listBuckets

AWS Managed (Predefined) Policies for CloudWatch Logs

AWS addresses many common use cases by providing standalone IAM policies that are created and administered by AWS. Managed policies grant necessary permissions for common use cases so you can avoid having to investigate what permissions are needed. For more information, see AWS Managed Policies in the *IAM User Guide*.

The following AWS managed policies, which you can attach to users in your account, are specific to CloudWatch Logs:

- **CloudWatchLogsFullAccess** – Grants full access to CloudWatch Logs.
- **CloudWatchLogsReadOnlyAccess** – Grants read-only access to CloudWatch Logs.

Note
You can review these permissions policies by signing in to the IAM console and searching for specific policies there.

You can also create your own custom IAM policies to allow permissions for CloudWatch Logs actions and resources. You can attach these custom policies to the IAM users or groups that require those permissions.

Customer Managed Policy Examples

In this section, you can find example user policies that grant permissions for various CloudWatch Logs actions. These policies work when you are using the CloudWatch Logs API, AWS SDKs, or the AWS CLI.

Topics

- Example 1: Allow Full Access to CloudWatch Logs
- Example 2: Allow Read-Only Access to CloudWatch Logs

Example 1: Allow Full Access to CloudWatch Logs

The following policy allows a user to access all CloudWatch Logs actions.

```
1  {
2    "Version": "2012-10-17",
3    "Statement": [
4      {
5        "Action": [
6          "logs:*"
7        ],
8        "Effect": "Allow",
9        "Resource": "*"
10     }
11   ]
12 }
```

Example 2: Allow Read-Only Access to CloudWatch Logs

The following policy allows a user read-only access to CloudWatch Logs data.

```json
1  {
2    "Version":"2012-10-17",
3    "Statement":[
4       {
5          "Action":[
6             "logs:Describe*",
7             "logs:Get*",
8             "logs:TestMetricFilter",
9             "logs:FilterLogEvents"
10         ],
11         "Effect":"Allow",
12         "Resource":"*"
13      }
14   ]
15 }
```

CloudWatch Logs Permissions Reference

When you are setting up Access Control and writing permissions policies that you can attach to an IAM identity (identity-based policies), you can use the following table as a reference. The table lists each CloudWatch Logs API operation and the corresponding actions for which you can grant permissions to perform the action. You specify the actions in the policy's `Action` field, and you specify a wildcard character (*) as the resource value in the policy's `Resource` field.

You can use AWS-wide condition keys in your CloudWatch Logs policies to express conditions. For a complete list of AWS-wide keys, see AWS Global and IAM Condition Context Keys in the *IAM User Guide*.

Note
To specify an action, use the `logs:` prefix followed by the API operation name. For example: `logs: CreateLogGroup`, `logs:CreateLogStream`, or `logs:*` (for all CloudWatch Logs actions).

CloudWatch Logs API Operations and Required Permissions for Actions

CloudWatch Logs API Operations	Required Permissions (API Actions)
CancelExportTask	`logs:CancelExportTask` Required to cancel a pending or running export task.
CreateExportTask	`logs:CreateExportTask` Required to export data from a log group to an Amazon S3 bucket.
CreateLogGroup	`logs:CreateLogGroup` Required to create a new log group.
CreateLogStream	`logs:CreateLogStream` Required to create a new log stream in a log group.
DeleteDestination	`logs:DeleteDestination` Required to delete a log destination and disables any subscription filters to it.
DeleteLogGroup	`logs:DeleteLogGroup` Required to delete a log group and any associated archived log events.
DeleteLogStream	`logs:DeleteLogStream` Required to delete a log stream and any associated archived log events.
DeleteMetricFilter	`logs:DeleteMetricFilter` Required to delete a metric filter associated with a log group.
DeleteRetentionPolicy	`logs:DeleteRetentionPolicy` Required to delete a log group's retention policy.
DeleteSubscriptionFilter	`logs:DeleteSubscriptionFilter` Required to delete the subscription filter associated with a log group.
DescribeDestinations	`logs:DescribeDestinations` Required to view all destinations associated with the account.
DescribeExportTasks	`logs:DescribeExportTasks` Required to view all export tasks associated with the account.
DescribeLogGroups	`logs:DescribeLogGroups` Required to view all log groups associated with the account.
DescribeLogStreams	`logs:DescribeLogStreams` Required to view all log streams associated with a log group.

CloudWatch Logs API Operations	Required Permissions (API Actions)
DescribeMetricFilters	`logs:DescribeMetricFilters` Required to view all metrics associated with a log group.
DescribeSubscriptionFilters	`logs:DescribeSubscriptionFilters` Required to view all subscription filters associated with a log group.
FilterLogEvents	`logs:FilterLogEvents` Required to sort log events by log group filter pattern.
GetLogEvents	`logs:GetLogEvents` Required to retrieve log events from a log stream.
ListTagsLogGroup	`logs:ListTagsLogGroup` Required to list the tags associated with a log group.
PutDestination	`logs:PutDestination` Required to create or update a destination log stream (such as an Kinesis stream).
PutDestinationPolicy	`logs:PutDestinationPolicy` Required to create or update an access policy associated with an existing log destination.
PutLogEvents	`logs:PutLogEvents` Required to upload a batch of log events to a log stream.
PutMetricFilter	`logs:PutMetricFilter` Required to create or update a metric filter and associate it with a log group.
PutRetentionPolicy	`logs:PutRetentionPolicy` Required to set the number of days to keep log events (retention) in a log group.
PutSubscriptionFilter	`logs:PutSubscriptionFilter` Required to create or update a subscription filter and associate it with a log group.
TagLogGroup	`logs:TagLogGroup` Required to add or update log group tags.
TestMetricFilter	`logs:TestMetricFilter` Required to test a filter pattern against a sampling of log event messages.

Using CloudWatch Logs with Interface VPC Endpoints

You can use an interface VPC endpoint to keep traffic between your Amazon VPC and CloudWatch Logs from leaving the Amazon network. Interface VPC endpoints don't require an internet gateway, NAT device, VPN connection, or AWS Direct Connect connection. Interface VPC endpoints are powered by AWS PrivateLink, an AWS technology that enables private communication between AWS services using an elastic network interface with private IP addresses in your Amazon VPC. For more information about Amazon VPC, see What is Amazon VPC in the *Amazon VPC User Guide*. For more information about AWS PrivateLink, see New – AWS PrivateLink for AWS Services.

To get started, create an interface VPC endpoint. You do not need to change the settings for CloudWatch Logs. CloudWatch Logs calls other AWS services using either public endpoints or private interface VPC endpoints, whichever are in use. For example, if you create an interface VPC endpoint for CloudWatch Logs, and you already have a CloudWatch Logs subscription filter for Kinesis Data Streams and an interface VPC endpoint for Kinesis Data Streams, calls between CloudWatch Logs and Kinesis Data Streams begin to flow through the interface VPC endpoint. For more information, see New – AWS PrivateLink for AWS Services.

Availability

CloudWatch Logs currently supports VPC endpoints in the following Regions:

- US West (Oregon)
- Asia Pacific (Tokyo);
- South America (São Paulo)

Logging Amazon CloudWatch Logs API Calls in AWS CloudTrail

AWS CloudTrail is a service that captures API calls made by or on behalf of your AWS account. This information is collected and written to CloudTrail log files that are stored in an Amazon S3 bucket that you specify. CloudTrail logs API calls whenever you use the API, the console, or the AWS CLI. Using the information collected by CloudTrail, you can determine what request was made, the source IP address the request was made from, who made the request, when it was made, and so on.

To learn more about CloudTrail, including how to configure and enable it, see the What is AWS CloudTrail in the *AWS CloudTrail User Guide.*

Topics

- CloudWatch Logs Information in CloudTrail
- Understanding Log File Entries

CloudWatch Logs Information in CloudTrail

If CloudTrail logging is turned on, calls made to API actions are captured in CloudTrail log files. Every log file entry contains information about who generated the request. For example, if a request is made to create a CloudWatch Logs log stream (`CreateLogStream`), CloudTrail logs the user identity of the person or service that made the request.

The user identity information in the log entry helps you determine the following:

- Whether the request was made with root or IAM user credentials
- Whether the request was made with temporary security credentials for a role or federated user
- Whether the request was made by another AWS service

For more information, see the CloudTrail userIdentity Element in the *AWS CloudTrail User Guide.*

You can store your CloudTrail log files in your S3 bucket for as long as you want, but you can also define Amazon S3 lifecycle rules to archive or delete log files automatically. By default, your log files are encrypted by using Amazon S3 server-side encryption (SSE).

If you want to be notified upon CloudTrail log file delivery, you can configure CloudTrail to publish Amazon SNS notifications when new log files are delivered. For more information, see Configuring Amazon SNS Notifications for CloudTrail in the *AWS CloudTrail User Guide.*

You can also aggregate CloudTrail log files from multiple AWS regions and multiple AWS accounts into a single S3 bucket. For more information, see Receiving CloudTrail Log Files from Multiple Regions and Receiving CloudTrail Log Files from Multiple Accounts in the *AWS CloudTrail User Guide.*

When logging is turned on, the request and response elements are logged in CloudTrail for these CloudWatch Logs API actions:

- CancelExportTask
- CreateExportTask
- CreateLogGroup
- CreateLogStream
- DeleteDestination
- DeleteLogGroup
- DeleteLogStream
- DeleteMetricFilter
- DeleteRetentionPolicy
- DeleteSubscriptionFilter
- PutDestination
- PutDestinationPolicy

- PutMetricFilter
- PutRetentionPolicy
- PutSubscriptionFilter
- TestMetricFilter

Only request elements are logged in CloudTrail for these CloudWatch Logs API actions:

- DescribeDestinations
- DescribeExportTasks
- DescribeLogGroups
- DescribeLogStreams
- DescribeMetricFilters
- DescribeSubscriptionFilters

The `GetLogEvents`, `PutLogEvents`, and `FilterLogEvents` CloudWatch Logs API actions are not supported.

For more information about the CloudWatch Logs actions, see the Amazon CloudWatch Logs API Reference.

Understanding Log File Entries

CloudTrail log files contain one or more log entries. Each entry lists multiple JSON-formatted events. A log entry represents a single request from any source and includes information about the requested action, the date and time of the action, request parameters, and so on. The log entries are not an ordered stack trace of the public API calls, so they do not appear in any specific order. Log file entries for all API actions are similar to the examples below.

The following log file entry shows that a user called the CloudWatch Logs **CreateExportTask** action.

```
1  {
2      "eventVersion": "1.03",
3      "userIdentity": {
4          "type": "IAMUser",
5          "principalId": "EX_PRINCIPAL_ID",
6          "arn": "arn:aws:iam::123456789012:user/someuser",
7          "accountId": "123456789012",
8          "accessKeyId": "AKIAIOSFODNN7EXAMPLE",
9          "userName": "someuser"
10     },
11     "eventTime": "2016-02-08T06:35:14Z",
12     "eventSource": "logs.amazonaws.com",
13     "eventName": "CreateExportTask",
14     "awsRegion": "us-east-1",
15     "sourceIPAddress": "127.0.0.1",
16     "userAgent": "aws-sdk-ruby2/2.0.0.rc4 ruby/1.9.3 x86_64-linux Seahorse/0.1.0",
17     "requestParameters": {
18         "destination": "yourdestination",
19         "logGroupName": "yourloggroup",
20         "to": 123456789012,
21         "from": 0,
22         "taskName": "yourtask"
23     },
24     "responseElements": {
25         "taskId": "15e5e534-9548-44ab-a221-64d9d2b27b9b"
26     },
27     "requestID": "1cd74c1c-ce2e-12e6-99a9-8dbb26bd06c9",
28     "eventID": "fd072859-bd7c-4865-9e76-8e364e89307c",
29     "eventType": "AwsApiCall",
```

```
30        "apiVersion": "20140328",
31        "recipientAccountId": "123456789012"
32 }
```

CloudWatch Logs Agent Reference

The CloudWatch Logs agent provides an automated way to send log data to CloudWatch Logs from Amazon EC2 instances. The agent is comprised of the following components:

- A plug-in to the AWS CLI that pushes log data to CloudWatch Logs.
- A script (daemon) that initiates the process to push data to CloudWatch Logs.
- A cron job that ensures that the daemon is always running.

Agent Configuration File

The CloudWatch Logs agent configuration file describes information needed by the CloudWatch Logs agent. The agent configuration file's [general] section defines common configurations that apply to all log streams. The [logstream] section defines the information necessary to send a local file to a remote log stream. You can have more than one [logstream] section, but each must have a unique name within the configuration file, e.g., [logstream1], [logstream2], and so on. The [logstream] value along with the first line of data in the log file, define the log file's identity.

```
1  [general]
2  state_file = value
3  logging_config_file = value
4  use_gzip_http_content_encoding = [true | false]
5
6  [logstream1]
7  log_group_name = value
8  log_stream_name = value
9  datetime_format = value
10 time_zone = [LOCAL|UTC]
11 file = value
12 file_fingerprint_lines = integer | integer-integer
13 multi_line_start_pattern = regex | {datetime_format}
14 initial_position = [start_of_file | end_of_file]
15 encoding = [ascii|utf_8|..]
16 buffer_duration = integer
17 batch_count = integer
18 batch_size = integer
19
20 [logstream2]
21 ...
```

state_file
Specifies where the state file is stored.

logging_config_file
(Optional) Specifies the location of the agent logging config file. If you do not specify an agent logging config file here, the default file awslogs.conf is used. The default file location is /var/awslogs/etc/awslogs.conf if you installed the agent with a script, and is /etc/awslogs/awslogs.conf if you installed the agent with rpm. The file is in Python configuration file format (https://docs/.python/.org/2/library/logging/.config/.html/#logging-config/-fileformat/)/. Loggers with the following names can be customized.

```
1  cwlogs.push
2  cwlogs.push.reader
3  cwlogs.push.publisher
4  cwlogs.push.event
5  cwlogs.push.batch
```

```
 6 cwlogs.push.stream
 7 cwlogs.push.watcher
```

The sample below changes the level of reader and publisher to WARNING while the default value is INFO.

```
 1 [loggers]
 2 keys=root,cwlogs,reader,publisher
 3
 4 [handlers]
 5 keys=consoleHandler
 6
 7 [formatters]
 8 keys=simpleFormatter
 9
10 [logger_root]
11 level=INFO
12 handlers=consoleHandler
13
14 [logger_cwlogs]
15 level=INFO
16 handlers=consoleHandler
17 qualname=cwlogs.push
18 propagate=0
19
20 [logger_reader]
21 level=WARNING
22 handlers=consoleHandler
23 qualname=cwlogs.push.reader
24 propagate=0
25
26 [logger_publisher]
27 level=WARNING
28 handlers=consoleHandler
29 qualname=cwlogs.push.publisher
30 propagate=0
31
32 [handler_consoleHandler]
33 class=logging.StreamHandler
34 level=INFO
35 formatter=simpleFormatter
36 args=(sys.stderr,)
37
38 [formatter_simpleFormatter]
39 format=%(asctime)s - %(name)s - %(levelname)s - %(process)d - %(threadName)s - %(message)s
```

use_gzip_http_content_encoding
When set to true (default), enables gzip http content encoding to send compressed payloads to CloudWatch Logs. This decreases CPU usage, lowers NetworkOut, and decreases put latency. To disable this feature, add **use_gzip_http_content_encoding = false** to the [**general**] section of the CloudWatch Logs agent configuration file, and then restart the agent.
This setting is only available in awscli-cwlogs version 1.3.3 and later.

log_group_name
Specifies the destination log group. A log group is created automatically if it doesn't already exist. Log group names can be between 1 and 512 characters long. Allowed characters include a-z, A-Z, 0-9, '_' (underscore), '-' (hyphen), '/' (forward slash), and '.' (period).

log_stream_name

Specifies the destination log stream. You can use a literal string or predefined variables ({instance_id}, {hostname}, {ip_address}), or combination of both to define a log stream name. A log stream is created automatically if it doesn't already exist.

datetime_format

Specifies how the timestamp is extracted from logs. The timestamp is used for retrieving log events and generating metrics. The current time is used for each log event if the **datetime_format** isn't provided. If the provided **datetime_format** value is invalid for a given log message, the timestamp from the last log event with a successfully parsed timestamp is used. If no previous log events exist, the current time is used.

The common datetime_format codes are listed below. You can also use any datetime_format codes supported by Python, datetime.strptime(). The timezone offset (%z) is also supported even though it's not supported until python 3.2, [+-]HHMM without colon(:). For more information, see strftime() and strptime() Behavior.

%y: Year without century as a zero-padded decimal number. 00, 01, ..., 99

%Y: Year with century as a decimal number.1970, 1988, 2001, 2013

%b: Month as locale's abbreviated name. Jan, Feb, ..., Dec (en_US);

%B: Month as locale's full name. January, February, ..., December (en_US);

%m: Month as a zero-padded decimal number. 01, 02, ..., 12

%d: Day of the month as a zero-padded decimal number. 01, 02, ..., 31

%H: Hour (24-hour clock) as a zero-padded decimal number. 00, 01, ..., 23

%I: Hour (12-hour clock) as a zero-padded decimal number. 01, 02, ..., 12

%p: Locale's equivalent of either AM or PM.

%M: Minute as a zero-padded decimal number. 00, 01, ..., 59

%S: Second as a zero-padded decimal number. 00, 01, ..., 59

%f: Microsecond as a decimal number, zero-padded on the left. 000000, ..., 999999

%z: UTC offset in the form +HHMM or -HHMM. +0000, -0400, +1030

Example formats:

Syslog: '%b %d %H:%M:%S', e.g. Jan 23 20:59:29

Log4j: '%d %b %Y %H:%M:%S', e.g. 24 Jan 2014 05:00:00

ISO8601: '%Y-%m-%dT%H:%M:%S%z', e.g. 2014-02-20T05:20:20+0000

time_zone

Specifies the time zone of log event timestamp. The two supported values are UTC and LOCAL. The default is LOCAL, which is used if time zone can't be inferred based on **datetime_format**.

file

Specifies log files that you want to push to CloudWatch Logs. File can point to a specific file or multiple files (using wildcards such as /var/log/system.log*). Only the latest file is pushed to CloudWatch Logs based on file modification time. We recommend that you use wildcards to specify a series of files of the same type, such as access_log.2014-06-01-01, access_log.2014-06-01-02, and so on, but not multiple kinds of files, such as access_log_80 and access_log_443. To specify multiple kinds of files, add another log stream entry to the configuration file so each kind of log file goes to a different log stream. Zipped files are not supported.

file_fingerprint_lines

Specifies the range of lines for identifying a file. The valid values are one number or two dash delimited numbers, such as '1', '2-5'. The default value is '1' so the first line is used to calculate fingerprint. Fingerprint lines are not sent to CloudWatch Logs unless all the specified lines are available.

multi_line_start_pattern

Specifies the pattern for identifying the start of a log message. A log message is made of a line that matches the pattern and any following lines that don't match the pattern. The valid values are regular expression or {datetime_format}. When using {datetime_format}, the datetime_format option should be specified. The default value is '^[^\s]' so any line that begins with non-whitespace character closes the previous log message and starts a new log message.

initial_position

Specifies where to start to read data (start_of_file or end_of_file). The default is start_of_file. It's only used if there is no state persisted for that log stream.

encoding

Specifies the encoding of the log file so that the file can be read correctly. The default is utf_8. Encodings supported by Python codecs.decode() can be used here.

Specifying an incorrect encoding might cause data loss because characters that cannot be decoded are replaced with some other character. Below are some common encodings:

```
ascii, big5, big5hkscs, cp037, cp424, cp437, cp500, cp720, cp737, cp775, cp850, cp852, cp855
, cp856, cp857, cp858, cp860, cp861, cp862, cp863, cp864, cp865, cp866, cp869, cp874, cp875,
 cp932, cp949, cp950, cp1006, cp1026, cp1140, cp1250, cp1251, cp1252, cp1253, cp1254, cp1255
, cp1256, cp1257, cp1258, euc_jp, euc_jis_2004, euc_jisx0213, euc_kr, gb2312, gbk, gb18030,
 hz, iso2022_jp, iso2022_jp_1, iso2022_jp_2, iso2022_jp_2004, iso2022_jp_3, iso2022_jp_ext
, iso2022_kr, latin_1, iso8859_2, iso8859_3, iso8859_4, iso8859_5, iso8859_6, iso8859_7,
iso8859_8, iso8859_9, iso8859_10, iso8859_13, iso8859_14, iso8859_15, iso8859_16, johab,
koi8_r, koi8_u, mac_cyrillic, mac_greek, mac_iceland, mac_latin2, mac_roman, mac_turkish,
ptcp154, shift_jis, shift_jis_2004, shift_jisx0213, utf_32, utf_32_be, utf_32_le, utf_16,
utf_16_be, utf_16_le, utf_7, utf_8, utf_8_sig
```

buffer_duration

Specifies the time duration for the batching of log events. The minimum value is 5000ms and default value is 5000ms.

batch_count

Specifies the max number of log events in a batch, up to 10000. The default value is 1000.

batch_size

Specifies the max size of log events in a batch, in bytes, up to 1048576 bytes. The default value is 32768 bytes. This size is calculated as the sum of all event messages in UTF-8, plus 26 bytes for each log event.

Using the CloudWatch Logs Agent with HTTP Proxies

You can use the CloudWatch Logs agent with HTTP proxies.

Note

HTTP proxies are supported in awslogs-agent-setup.py version 1.3.8 or later.

To use the CloudWatch Logs agent with HTTP proxies

1. Do one of the following:

    1. For a new installation of the CloudWatch Logs agent, run the following commands:

       ```
       1 curl https://s3.amazonaws.com/aws-cloudwatch/downloads/latest/awslogs-agent-setup.py -O
       ```

       ```
       1 sudo python awslogs-agent-setup.py --region us-east-1 --http-proxy http://your/proxy --
           https-proxy http://your/proxy --no-proxy 169.254.169.254
       ```

       In order to maintain access to the Amazon EC2 metadata service on EC2 instances, use **--no-proxy 169.254.169.254** (recommended). For more information, see Instance Metadata and User Data in the *Amazon EC2 User Guide for Linux Instances*.

       In the values for `http-proxy` and `https-proxy`, you specify the entire URL.

    2. For an existing installation of the CloudWatch Logs agent, edit /var/awslogs/etc/proxy.conf, and add your proxies:

       ```
       1 HTTP_PROXY=
       2 HTTPS_PROXY=
       3 NO_PROXY=
       ```

2. Restart the agent for the changes to take effect:

```
1 sudo service awslogs restart
```

If you are using Amazon Linux 2, use the following command to restart the agent:

```
1 sudo service awslogsd restart
```

Compartmentalizing CloudWatch Logs Agent Configuration Files

If you're using awslogs-agent-setup.py version 1.3.8 or later with awscli-cwlogs 1.3.3 or later, you can import different stream configurations for various components independently of one another by creating additional configuration files in the **/var/awslogs/etc/config/** directory. When the CloudWatch Logs agent starts, it includes any stream configurations in these additional configuration files. Configuration properties in the [general] section must be defined in the main configuration file (/var/awslogs/etc/awslogs.conf) and are ignored in any additional configuration files found in /var/awslogs/etc/config/.

If you don't have a **/var/awslogs/etc/config/** directory because you installed the agent with rpm, you can use the **/etc/awslogs/config/** directory instead.

Restart the agent for the changes to take effect:

```
1 sudo service awslogs restart
```

If you are using Amazon Linux 2, use the following command to restart the agent:

```
1 sudo service awslogsd restart
```

CloudWatch Logs Agent FAQs

What kinds of file rotations are supported?

The following file rotation mechanisms are supported:

- Renaming existing log files with a numerical suffix, then re-creating the original empty log file. For example, /var/log/syslog.log is renamed /var/log/syslog.log.1. If /var/log/syslog.log.1 already exists from a previous rotation, it is renamed /var/log/syslog.log.2.
- Truncating the original log file in place after creating a copy. For example, /var/log/syslog.log is copied to /var/log/syslog.log.1 and /var/log/syslog.log is truncated. There might be data loss for this case, so be careful about using this file rotation mechanism.
- Creating a new file with a common pattern as the old one. For example, /var/log/syslog.log.2014-01-01 remains and /var/log/syslog.log.2014-01-02 is created. The fingerprint (source ID) of the file is calculated by hashing the log stream key and the first line of file content. To override this behavior, the **file_fingerprint_lines** option can be used. When file rotation happens, the new file is supposed to have new content and the old file is not supposed to have content appended; the agent pushes the new file after it finishes reading the old file.

How can I determine which version of agent am I using?

If you used a setup script to install the CloudWatch Logs agent, you can use **/var/awslogs/bin/awslogs-version.sh** to check what version of the agent you are using. It prints out the version of the agent and its major dependencies. If you used yum to install the CloudWatch Logs agent, you can use "**yum info awslogs**" and "**yum info aws-cli-plugin-cloudwatch-logs**" to check the version of the CloudWatch Logs agent and plugin.

How are log entries converted to log events?

Log events contain two properties: the timestamp of when the event occurred, and the raw log message. By default, any line that begins with non-whitespace character closes the previous log message if there is one, and starts a new log message. To override this behavior, the **multi_line_start_pattern** can be used and any line that matches the pattern starts a new log message. The pattern could be any regex or '{datetime_format}'.

For example, if the first line of every log message contains a timestamp like '2014-01-02T13:13:01Z', then the **multi_line_start_pattern** can be set to '\d{4}-\d{2}-\d{2}T\d{2}:\d{2}:\d{2}Z'. To simplify the configuration, the '{datetime_format}' variable can be used if the **datetime_format option** is specified. For the same example, if **datetime_format** is set to '%Y-%m-%dT%H:%M:%S%z', then multi_line_start_pattern could be simply '{datetime_format}'.

The current time is used for each log event if the **datetime_format** isn't provided. If the provided **datetime_format** is invalid for a given log message, the timestamp from the last log event with a successfully parsed timestamp is used. If no previous log events exist, the current time is used. A warning message is logged when a log event falls back to the current time or time of previous log event.

Timestamps are used for retrieving log events and generating metrics, so if you specify the wrong format, log events could become non-retrievable and generate wrong metrics.

How are log events batched?

A batch becomes full and is published when any of the following conditions are met:

1. The **buffer_duration** amount of time has passed since the first log event was added.

2. Less than **batch_size** of log events have been accumulated but adding the new log event exceeds the **batch_size**.

3. The number of log events has reached **batch_count**.

4. Log events from the batch don't span more than 24 hours, but adding the new log event exceeds the 24 hours constraint.

What would cause log entries, log events, or batches to be skipped or truncated?

To follow the constraint of the `PutLogEvents` operation, the following issues could cause a log event or batch to be skipped.

The CloudWatch Logs agent writes a warning to its log when data is skipped.

1. If the size of a log event exceeds 256 KB, the log event is skipped completely.

2. If the timestamp of log event is more than 2 hours in future, the log event is skipped.

3. If the timestamp of log event is more than 14 days in past, the log event is skipped.

4. If any log event is older than the retention period of log group, the whole batch is skipped.

5. If the batch of log events in a single `PutLogEvents` request spans more than 24 hours, the `PutLogEvents` operation fails.

Does stopping the agent cause data loss/duplicates?

Not as long as the state file is available and no file rotation has happened since the last run. The CloudWatch Logs agent can start from where it stopped and continue pushing the log data.

Can I point different log files from the same or different hosts to the same log stream?

Configuring multiple log sources to send data to a single log stream is not supported.

What API calls does the agent make (or what actions should I add to my IAM policy)?

The CloudWatch Logs agent requires the `CreateLogGroup`, `CreateLogStream`, `DescribeLogStreams`, and `PutLogEvents` operations. If you're using the latest agent, `DescribeLogStreams` is not needed. See the sample IAM policy below.

```
1 {
2 "Version": "2012-10-17",
3 "Statement": [
4   {
5     "Effect": "Allow",
6     "Action": [
7       "logs:CreateLogGroup",
8       "logs:CreateLogStream",
9       "logs:PutLogEvents",
```

```
10        "logs:DescribeLogStreams"
11      ],
12      "Resource": [
13        "arn:aws:logs:*:*:*"
14      ]
15    }
16  ]
17 }
```

I don't want the CloudWatch Logs agent to create either log groups or log streams automatically. How can I prevent the agent from recreating both log groups and log streams?
In your IAM policy, you can restrict the agent to only the following operations: DescribeLogStreams, PutLogEvents.

What logs should I look at when troubleshooting?
The agent installation log is at /var/log/awslogs-agent-setup.log and the agent log is at /var/log/awslogs.log.

Document History

The following table describes the important changes to the Amazon CloudWatch Logs User's Guide.

Change	Description	Release Date
Interface VPC endpoints	In some regions, you can use an interface VPC endpoint to keep traffic between your Amazon VPC and CloudWatch Logs from leaving the Amazon network. For more information see Using CloudWatch Logs with Interface VPC Endpoints.	7 March 2018
Route 53 DNS query logs	You can use CloudWatch Logs to store logs about the DNS queries received by Route 53. For more information see What is Amazon CloudWatch Logs? or Logging DNS Queries in the Amazon Route 53 Developer Guide.	7 September 2017
Tag log groups	You can use tags to categorize your log groups. For more information, see Tag Log Groups in Amazon CloudWatch Logs.	13 December 2016
Console improvements	You can navigate from metrics graphs to the associated log groups. For more information, see Pivot from Metrics to Logs.	7 November 2016
Console usability improvements	Improved the experience to make it easier to search, filter, and troubleshoot. For example, you can now filter your log data to a date and time range. For more information, see View Log Data Sent to CloudWatch Logs.	29 August 2016
Added AWS CloudTrail support for Amazon CloudWatch Logs and new CloudWatch Logs metrics	Added AWS CloudTrail support for CloudWatch Logs. For more information, see Logging Amazon CloudWatch Logs API Calls in AWS CloudTrail.	10 March 2016
Added support for CloudWatch Logs export to Amazon S3	Added support for exporting CloudWatch Logs data to Amazon S3. For more information, see Exporting Log Data to Amazon S3.	7 December 2015

Change	Description	Release Date
Added support for AWS CloudTrail logged events in Amazon CloudWatch Logs	You can create alarms in CloudWatch and receive notifications of particular API activity as captured by CloudTrail and use the notification to perform troubleshooting.	November 10, 2014
Added support for Amazon CloudWatch Logs	You can use Amazon CloudWatch Logs to monitor, store, and access your system, application, and custom log files from Amazon Elastic Compute Cloud (Amazon EC2) instances or other sources. You can then retrieve the associated log data from CloudWatch Logs using the Amazon CloudWatch console, the CloudWatch Logs commands in the AWS CLI, or the CloudWatch Logs SDK. For more information, see What is Amazon CloudWatch Logs?.	July 10, 2014

AWS Glossary

For the latest AWS terminology, see the AWS Glossary in the *AWS General Reference*.

www.ingramcontent.com/pod-product-compliance
Lightning Source LLC
LaVergne TN
LVHW082040050326
832904LV00005B/246